"All the world's a stage." ~ *William Shakespeare*

Volume Two

JOURNEY
TO THE
STAGE

Compiled and Presented by
Women's Prosperity Network

ParkerHouseBooks.com

Book design: Candi Parker
Editing: Judee Light
Published by ParkerHouseBooks.com

This book is available at quantity discounts for bulk purchases and for branding by businesses and organizations. For further information or to learn more about Women's Prosperity Network, contact Team@WomensProsperityNetwork.com or call (800) 928-6928.

Praise for Journey to the Stage

AWESOME!!!

"So many inspiring stories in this book. These women are truly motivating! I love reading this book and receiving so many wonderful nuggets to help me in my business and in my life."

~ Shannon LeBlanc

Get inspiration to get on the Stage!

"Reading each person's journey to the stage is fantastic. The individuality of each story is so unique and inspiring at the same time. Speaking in public is one of the scariest events many of us can imagine; knowing that we are not alone in this and reading how others chose to get beyond their fears is motivating."

~ Ellen McDowell

Five Stars

"Inspiring stories these authors share about their journeys in life." *~ John Epstein*

Step up and speak it. Fantastic read!

"As a women who just found her voice in the last 5 years, I can honestly say that speaking has been the hardest thing to do. This book brings together powerful voices with the intention of empowering others to step up and speak their message. Kudos to the authors in Journey to the Stage who have shined a very bright light on stepping up and shining."

~ Carla Wynn Hall

They made me believe it can happen.

"Page after page, story after story, women and men sharing how they overcame obstacles that had previously kept them from their greatness. Some weren't even aware they had life-changing messages to share. This book has inspired me to stretch, to reach and to begin my own journey to greatness."

~ LaRonda Robinson

Contributing Authors

Jo Ann Goldsmith
Dr. Hepsharat Amadi
Abigail K. Hunter
Angie LeBlanc
Debra Melillo
Elin Mayer
Ellen McDowell
Catherine M. Laub
Melissa Binkley
Howard "Lucky" Luckman
Adele Alexandre
Ken Course
Velma Alford
Lauri Hunter
Marie Cantone
Sheril Jalm
Mark Moyou
Mery N. Dominguez
Nansi Coughlin
Leslie Warren
Regena Ozeryansky
Sherry Kane
Vismaya Rubin

About Women's Prosperity Network

Nancy Matthews, Trish Carr and Susan Wiener are three sisters (yes, real sisters with the same mother and the same father!) They founded Women's Prosperity Network in 2008 fueled by their passion and deep desire for women to recognize and embrace their own greatness and to honor the greatness in each other. They encourage and empower women to "Be Real, Get Real & Achieve Real Results" through ongoing mastermind sessions, workshops and seminars.

Since 2008 they have served over 10,000 women and men through a continuing community of support providing inspiration, education and a network of dynamic connections.

Their vision is a global community of impassioned, determined women, committed to supporting each other's pursuit of excellence and significantly impacting our world.

To learn more about Women's Prosperity Network (yes, men are invited too!), go to:

WomensProsperityNetwork.com

Email: Team@WomensProsperityNetwork.com

Phone: (800) 928-6928

Foreword by Nancy Matthews

On the first day of my public speaking class as a sophomore in college I sat towards the back of the class with more than just butterflies in my stomach. It was as if the butterflies were trying to escape from my body and the fear and anxiety had made their way from my tummy to my mouth, causing an overwhelming feeling of nausea. As I heard the professor describe the course outline with each of us having to deliver up to 10 presentations during the semester, I prayed the nausea wouldn't get so bad that I'd have to rush out to the bathroom or worse yet, toss my cookies right then and there!

Thankfully I made it through the class without that horrifying embarrassment and made the decision that I wouldn't have to suffer any type of embarrassment in that class because I was dropping it – and drop it I did.

Fast forward to this day, when I have the privilege of speaking all over the world, I thoroughly enjoy each and every presentation and feel giddy that this extraordinary joy is even called work.

The time in between that frightening moment in class and the delight I now feel every time I am asked to speak has been a journey filled with faith, fear, courage and a deep desire to add value to the lives of others.

You are about to embark on a journey where inspired and committed individuals have stepped up and stepped out, beyond the confines of their comfort zones, to share their messages in a bigger way. The authors share their truths, their fears, their challenges and most of all their passion for making a difference in their place on the world's stage.

May their stories inspire, encourage and empower you to embrace your own journey to the stage wherever that may be.

To Your Success, Peace & Prosperity,

Nancy Matthews
International Speaker, Best-Selling Author & Global Leader
Founder, Women's Prosperity Network

Table of Contents

Jo Ann Goldsmith, BFA, MSC, is the President of AuthenticBrandingWithHeart.com, a design and branding firm dedicated to creating Madison Avenue design with heart. She crafts exceptional advertising, logos and inspired illustration that attract, serve and support you to reach new levels of high impact corporate identity, sales and profit. Unique to Ms. Goldsmith's style is the integration of business visions and goals in harmony with the unspoken and intended essence of your heart and soul, magnetizing and attracting your perfect customers. Jo Ann is also a published Author, and has over 100 globally published illustrations that reflect her authenticity, heart and soul.

You can contact Jo Ann at: (561) 494-4326, creategoldmines@gmail.com, AuthenticBrandingWithHeart.com, or LinkedIn: Jo Ann Goldsmith | Design Branding Expert | MADISON AVENUE DESIGN WITH SOUL: Exceptional Advertising, Logos & Inspired Illustration.

An Unlikely Swan ~
A Journey of Transformation from
Ugly Duckling to Swan to Stage

Jo Ann Goldsmith

"You are a swan," a voice declared.

The words had come into my consciousness clearly during a morning ritual. Until that day, the word "swan" had never been used in my day-to-day vocabulary.

Immediately, I questioned it..."Me, a swan?" I say. If the voice had said, "You're an Ugly Duckling," I would have instantly agreed. But the voice persisted, so I jotted it down in my journal.

Two weeks later I would begin writing this story.

Months earlier, during another morning meditation, I saw a clear vision of myself on stage for the first time, speaking to a group of women in Hawaii. I was sharing my unique gifts, making a difference in their lives and I could feel the radiant energy of it. I knew I was being called to step up.

After many years of believing I would always be the Ugly Duckling, my journey to the stage had finally begun. Could it be that I would take the stage as a Swan?

My parents were both amazingly gifted. My mother was a world renowned Painter and my father was a Civil Engineer Steel Expert. They were talented, dedicated and hardworking, yet were never truly acknowledged for their talents. My younger brother was the apple of my mother's eye. So, even under the best of circumstances, I was second best. My freckles and frizzy hair didn't help my self-esteem either.

With hopes that people might eventually appreciate me more, I created my road map of reading between the lines, sensing the unseen, coming from heart, and striving to make a difference. By 10th grade, I knew that I had to figure out what I wanted to "BE." Academia was not for me, and a career in Art was looking better and better, despite the fact that I was living in my mother's shadow.

On a quest to find my own style and expression, I dabbled with different materials and tools. I discovered that, as long as I was in creation mode, delivering top-notch quality, I was happy. I became fascinated by advertising artwork—how some pictures, in conjunction with words, elicited feelings and a call to action. I dreamed of attending Syracuse University's prestigious Newhouse School of Communication to major in Advertising and Marketing. Never expecting to be accepted, I submitted my portfolio anyway. You can imagine my delight when I was handpicked!

Fueled by my passion and absolute determination, I consistently delivered projects that brought me to the top of my class, in spite of my Master Professor's criticisms.

"Just quit," he told me. "You're too sensitive. You'll never survive Madison Avenue."

When I graduated from S.U. with my BFA, I felt seen for the first time. Over one third of my graduating class had quit or flunked out. I landed my first Advertising Job at Dancer Fitzgerald Sample (DFS), on Madison Avenue in New York City, and I loved it. In my six years with DFS, I created national campaigns for Hanes Pantyhose, Duncan Hines Chocolate Chip Cookie Mix, Stove Top Stuffing for Chicken, Johnson & Johnson's New Product Home Division, just to name a few. My Massengill Douche Ad won a Clio Finalist Award. My transformation was continuing.

Confident in my environment at the time, I stretched my wings. My curiosity, and my desire to connect with people in a deeper way led me to spiritual pursuits, and I became a Minister of Spiritual Counseling. This was an unlikely choice for this Jewish girl from Great Neck, Long Island, so I kept my coaching and professional lives separate.

For the years that followed, I delighted in working both for the Madison Avenue agencies and with entrepreneurs. Top-notch photography shoots, models, generous budgets, stylists, and long lunches were all part of this exciting life. And, I loved working with my freelance clients, delivering Madison Avenue branding that they never would have been able to afford. That felt really good!

My diligence brought me recognition for my ads and storyboard illustrations. And, as if by accident, I earned the title of International Illustrator, too, when Paul Karasik chose me to create 23 unique corporate illustrations for his globally distributed business book, *Sweet Persuasion: the Illustrated Art of Closing a Sale.*

Through a series of traumatic life-changing events, my Madison Avenue advertising life came to an abrupt halt. In my first major move ever, I landed in Florida. Everything I knew was stripped away. Using all my intuitive gifts, and encouraged by women of heart who believed in me, I created branding with feeling. This time, without the "rules" of Madison Avenue, my designs flowed even more beautifully, beyond the images themselves. Suddenly, I was serving entrepreneurs who were having definitive bottom line results. And from that, my core business tagline emerged: "Hire this Goldsmith to Create Goldmines." I was an "Expert." Yet, I had not truly let go of my Ugly Duckling persona.

JoAnna Brandi, Certified Joy Coach, invited me to illustrate *54 Ways to Stay Positive*. With the birth of our book, intertwining words and 72 guided Illustrations, I finally caught a glimpse of my grand vision, my "WHY." Seeing people happy and beginning to live their visions as a result of reading our book made me feel joyful and fulfilled.

Slowly, I settled into a new Florida life that included wonderful friendships, clients, employment as a Creative Director for 10 Years, and a blessed marriage of the heart for 14 very special years. Then suddenly, four years ago, my beloved husband passed away. Alone again, my life changed abruptly. It took every lesson and gift I had ever received to spring forth with resiliency and heart. Who was I? A duckling? Or, a Swan?

Woody Allen said, "Eighty percent of success is showing up." So last December, when a dear friend told me about a "WOW Wednesday" call with featured guest, Ron Thiessen, I showed up. "Set your GPS to one business," he said. ONE? I had SEVEN business scenarios that had evolved since my husband's passing. Afraid, but wanting guidance, I bravely asked Ron his advice about my 7 "Rays." There was silence. I held my breath.

"Wow, you're a one stop shop!" he responded. "If I have branding needs, you do them. If I'm getting in my own way, you can take care of that too, and ..." He went through the whole list. And then he added, "You're very special."

Knock me over with a feather! I had been publicly acknowledged for doing everything right by a professional who saw the Swan in me.

And that got me thinking. Because of my stick-to-it-ive-ness and tenacity, I had almost always accomplished everything I focused on doing. Still, I hesitated to step into the limelight. My glass ceiling had always been to stop at #2. My lack of confidence held me back. My vision was calling me to step up. Could I do it?

Up until now, I'd done my business totally alone. And despite my many successes, part of me secretly felt that I might not be measuring up. But, a light bulb went on for me: if one WOW Wednesday call could make this much of a difference for me, what else might be possible with the support of a full network, or even a coach?

This first jump was the hardest. Attending the Women's Prosperity Network's Level Up Workshop, I reconnected to my vision to create powerful brand messaging with heart and soul. I jumped into creating renewed branding for myself. With the help of wonderful mentors and dear friends, I began stretching and becoming more open and accountable. Putting aside my Ugly Duckling persona, I committed to consistently and authentically showing up, just as I am.

What a novel idea! Black feathers or white feathers, Duckling or Swan, part of what I learned is that it takes more effort to stay in a place of negativity and not knowing, than it does to stand up and say, "I AM."

Today, I am stepping onto the stage, creating my vision to make a difference in the lives of Ugly Ducklings like me, so that they can serve the world, be themselves, be special, and be Swans. My goal is to inspire people of heart, and to capture their unique essence with my authentic branding. Together, we can create a visual representation of that which is seen and unseen. For when true magnetism is achieved, we all become part of the miraculous ripple effect that serves our combined higher purpose.

Supported and encouraged to look into the mirror, together we can finally see our reflections as the Swans we have always been, but never could see.

Acknowledging the support of all my wonderful mentors, and to Women's Prosperity Network, I say "thank you," especially to Nancy Matthews, my amazing Coach, who walked by my side with heart and knowingness, and who saw, and awoke the Swan in me.

It is my prayer for you that you step into your own spotlight and allow yourself to shine, glide and be the Swan of your own dreams.

Dr. Hepsharat Amadi is a native of New York, who graduated from Bronx High School of Science in 1974, Harvard University in 1979, State University of New York at Stony Brook Medical School in 1987 and Bronx-Lebanon Hospital Family Practice Residency in 1990. She moved to South Florida in 1990, graduated from the Community School of Traditional Chinese Health Care in 1998, and has been in solo private practice since 2001, doing holistic health care, including Quantum Bio-Feedback and Bio-Identical Hormone Replacement Therapy. She is married with three children.

You can contact her at: 954-757-0064 (office) and www.dramadi.com.

How and Why I Became a Speaker on Holistic Health

Dr. Hepsharat Amadi

I never saw myself as a speaker, but Life has many strange surprises in store for us! I never originally envisioned myself working in my own medical practice either, but rather assumed, as I made my way through medical school and residency, that I would be an employee, working in a clinic owned by someone else. However, it was my own view of what holistic medicine should really be all about that eventually led both to my becoming self-employed and becoming a speaker.

When I was around 15 years old, I was considering what I wanted to do for a career. I loved dance and had taken many dance lessons and performed with some amateur dance companies in New York City, where I grew up. But I was also fascinated by living beings and their physiology and psychology. I eventually decided to pursue medicine, instead of dance, as a career—for two reasons, one of which in retrospect was correct and the other perhaps not so correct. One main reason I chose medicine over dance was because I felt that in medicine I had a chance to get progressively better with age, whereas with dance, one's abilities as a performer tend to decrease as one's age advances. I still consider this to be true.

10

The other reason (which I was thinking at that time was accurate, but turned out not to be as true as I had thought then) was that, as an artist of any type, one's ability to earn a good living had to do with whether your audience understood and appreciated your work. I thought then that, at least with becoming a doctor, people would automatically understand what I did, so therefore there would be no appreciation of my artistry required in order for me to support myself, and maybe eventually, a family. Little did I know then that the medicine I would ultimately practice would be as much an art form as a science and that a lot of people might still not understand my art!

Before I even entered medical school, I knew that medications and surgery were not the basis of health. They were something useful for when a person's health had reached such a stage of imbalance that they needed to be stabilized, but they did not, in and of themselves, increase a person's level of health. I understood then that a person's health was determined by many factors: primarily their thoughts and emotions and the lifestyle habits that followed from those. However, at the time I entered medical school (in 1983), the medical school I attended didn't even have a course in nutrition, although it had a mandatory year-long rigorous course in pharmacology, which if you didn't pass, you didn't graduate. Offerings by my medical school and residency in training in psychology were relatively sporadic and cursory throughout my training, although I chose to pursue Family Practice, which had a bit more training in psychology than other specialties, with the exception of Psychiatry itself.

Graduating from Family Practice Residency in 1990, I

moved to South Florida, where I worked for several years associated with the University of Miami's Family Practice residency and working at Jackson Memorial Hospital's Urgent Care Center before leaving the academic environment to work in a series of private clinics. By then I had married and shortly after moving to Miami, had my first child. In 1994, I had a second child, which caused me to interrupt the acupuncture studies I had begun at The Community School of Traditional Chinese Health Care, while working full-time during the day at a clinic. The reason I decided to study acupuncture at that point, with an already demanding schedule what with full-time work and two young children, was because I saw how beautifully and quickly acupuncture helped to heal my husband of ulcer symptoms he was having at that time. In just one treatment, his symptoms were reduced by about 70% (which antacid medication had not been able to achieve), and within three treatments, his symptoms were completely gone and never returned for more than 10 years! I decided I needed to learn this type of medicine sooner rather than later, so that I would have something other than drugs and surgery to offer my patients!

It was in 1995, while working part-time as the staff doctor at the Hippocrates Health Institute in West Palm Beach, that I first began to do any "public speaking". I have heard that many people are extremely reluctant to speak in public, and I was no exception to that rule! However, I had to overcome that anxiety through repetition in front of small groups of people. People would come to stay at the institute, usually for three weeks at a time, so every three weeks I would have to get up in front of a new group of residents to introduce myself, give a little information about my background and entertain questions from the group. When I first started doing this, I would get really nervous just before I had to stand up and speak, but over the course of time, the shock wore off and I found myself actually enjoying the experience!

In May of 2001, I wound up leaving the situation of being an employee, after an employer that I was working for at the time, bounced a month's worth of my salary checks. I had given him a deadline of May 1st, 2001, to pay me the money he owed me or I would have to leave his employ. When that day came around and I could see that he had no intention of making good on his obligation, I was faced with three alternatives: (1) keep working for him in his clinic, hoping that he would change his behavior and start paying me in checks that cashed (unrealistic, to say the least!), (2) leave his employ to seek a new employer with possibly all the constraints and disappointments that previous employment situations had entailed or (3) strike out on my own, with no prior business experience or acumen, and no savings. Having had the experience of working for other people and institutions from the time I graduated from residency in 1990 up until May of 2001, I finally decided to take a chance on working for myself and being my own boss in terms of clinical decisions, without having to take direction from administrators who knew less about medicine than I did.

So there I was, in May of 2001, 10 months after the birth of my third and last child, with no job and no savings. Fortunately, a chiropractor friend of mine had encouraged me to start a part-time private practice sharing office space with her, which she kindly allowed me to use for free at first, and then with a sliding scale rent, as I built up my practice.

With the decision made to become self-employed, I went full-time with it, and gradually my practice grew, through word of mouth, and through advertising in one magazine only, that being one that was distributed free in health food stores. I figured the kind of people who shop in health food stores were the kind of people I wanted to be dealing with: those who recognized that their health was their own responsibility and who were willing to invest their money in nutritious food and the most natural health care. At that time, I was primarily doing lifestyle counseling, acupuncture, supplements and herbal medicine, but in 2003 I was introduced to Quantum Bio-Feedback, which became the main method by which I assessed and treated my patients.

Quantum Bio-Feedback is a way of assessing and treating what is going on with a person at the electromagnetic level. This is the level at which all change begins. Electromagnetic interactions govern biochemical reactions, and biochemical reactions ultimately determine the physical structure of a patient's body. In conventional Western medicine, electromagnetic function is virtually ignored, except in the case of the heart, where it is monitored using the EKG machine, and the brain, whose electrical functioning (i.e., brain waves) is monitored using an EEG machine. The Quantum Bio-feedback is a machine by which a person's entire electromagnetic functioning can be not only monitored, but improved, through treatment utilizing the machine. Here was an instrument which could improve health in a stable patient without using drugs or surgery! I also began using the machine to determine if a patient could benefit from bio-identical hormone therapy and what their best prescription for bio-identical hormones should be, which I found was a far more accurate indicator of what they needed than just blood or saliva tests alone.

As I said in the beginning, I never set out to speak from the stage or to have my own private practice. But following my passion has led me to both things. I honed my practice in speaking through my earlier part-time employment at Hippocrates, from business networking groups where I would have to stand and give my three-minute "commercial" about my business, and from addressing auditoriums full of people at health fairs at the Broward County Convention Center. Each time I get up in front of a group these days, whether large or small, I feel my heart starting to beat more rapidly and get that little shot of adrenaline, but as I warm into my talk, speaking straight from my experience and from my heart, the fright goes away, and I am left with just excitement and joy! As I make the connection with my audience, look them in the eyes, cause them to think about their health differently than they might ever have thought about it before, I wonder not only who out of this crowd might become a new patient of mine, but also whose life might I be helping to save with the information that they hear from me today?

"You are always in the right place at the right time ... the difference maker is the right attitude, choices and actions."
~Susan Wiener

Abigail K. Hunter, from Tallahassee, Florida, is the eldest of two children, with a younger brother, and the daughter of Lauri Hunter. Abigail is the CEO of her company, *Completely You!,* which enhances and embraces your fitness, fashion and faith, so you can be the unique, complete triple threat that you were born to be! She uses her undergraduate degree in Psychology to listen and connect with her clients. Abigail has a heart for community outreach and community service, which she puts into action through various organizations and independently paying it forward. Being one of the youngest members of Women's Prosperity Network, she appreciates and loves to learn from all the wisdom that surrounds her.

You can contact Abigail at: akhsuccess@gmail.com
Instagram @ab.k_   Twitter @ab_k_
www.completeyouwithabigail.tumblr.com
and Facebook Abigail Hunter.

The New Triple Threat...
Fashion, Fitness and Faith!

Abigail K. Hunter

It all started on the side of a cafeteria stage, when I was discreetly gasping for air after peeking from behind the curtains and seeing the cafeteria filled with the whole elementary school body, parents, and school staff as I was up next to give my presidential campaign speech, being a candidate for school president. Coming from a family that believes in doing things with excellence, I had gone over this speech a plethora of times and felt I had a good flow with it. However, that was in the comfort of my own home in front of my family. In seconds, I had to take the stage in front of my friends and peers that could judge me, and I knew I had to lead by example and show them I had the qualities to represent this student body with utmost confidence and respect.

Within seconds of being called to take the stage, I transformed into the most courageous and personable 10-year-old that I knew how to be, owning the words that came out of my mouth and going for what I wanted. From that point on, after serving as president of my school that year, I had a feeling that public speaking would somehow tag along with me throughout my life.

As I continued to grow and participate in different extracurricular activities such as sports, school talent shows and church plays, I began to notice that being on stage and in front of people wasn't half bad. I was always nervous before I got on stage, but found a happy place in performing and began to notice how that didn't happen for everybody.

Throughout the cultivation of my life in grade school, with there not being much of a need for me to speak publicly, speaking took a back seat to everything else that I was involved in, which involved physical rather than verbal activity. Yet speaking came back out when need be for an occasional class speech in order to get the grade I needed.

As I continued through school, my freshman year in college came along and I received a call from a church member who was a teacher at my old elementary school at the time, asking me to be one of the commencement speakers for the fifth grade graduation. I looked up to the sky, smiled and said, "You're funny." It's crazy how God works and how, as a child, little did I know He was preparing me for this very moment. I said, "Yes," and had the pleasure of sharing the stage with state representatives and community leaders.

There is an estimated four-year period of time that some people experience, where you gain unforgettable memories, find lifelong friends, earn a degree that you may or may not put to use and, if you're lucky, owe Sallie Mae half of your income in the future. That place is called college. Throughout my time in college, I had the desire to learn more about myself and to find my purpose on this earth. Well, that was easier said than done and little did I know, throughout that search, a lot of my learning would come from outside of the classroom.

Being athletic, I continued to work out while in college, but I found that it wasn't easy. It was very hard to catch the odd hours of the student gym, and the track was always closed due to the football team hogging it. It was a hassle. If workout equipment was available as much as the food options in the cafeteria, "Freshman 15" would be nonexistent. So I had to get creative and learn how to improvise. I lived in a dorm that had 12 floors, so I began to run the steps every night before bed and do a few exercises in my room, and my friends began to join me. I then found out that I had a love for helping others take care of their bodies. Slowly but surely, I was filling in the pieces of this puzzle called *self,* and fitness was the first piece.

You know how you have a passion for something, but you don't know it could be a valuable quality that could potentially add to your income? Well, that's how fashion is for me. I remember my mother telling me, "As soon as you could recognize clothes, you knew what you wanted and didn't want." I've always had a passion for fashion. I wasn't shaped like the average little girl. I always had a curvy and athletic figure which at one point in time was very hard for me to shop for. I didn't understand why the same dress would work for my friends but not for me. It wasn't until I got a little older that my mom schooled me on how certain types of clothing worked for certain body types. That was the starting point for my interest in fashion. I enjoyed learning that cinching the waist worked well for a pear shape and how a peplum skirt worked for a straight figure. I then began to help others around me. Another piece added to the puzzle.

During this time of finding myself, I didn't negate the

incredible things that I learned in the classroom. I love the study of the mind and mental processes, and that's why psychology was the perfect fit for me. I graduated with a Bachelor's degree in Psychology and then faced the harsh reality and big question that a lot of fresh college graduates ask themselves: "Where do I go from here?"

I had found some pieces of my puzzle, but had no earthly idea how they fit together. Shortly after graduating, I attended Loral Langemeier's Millionaire Summit along with my mother and brother. At the beginning of the trip, I was just going to get out of town and spend time with my brother before he headed back to college. This summit was the first big conference that my brother and I had attended.

After the first day of the summit, my mind was blown! I was so full with the knowledge that I received from the guest speakers. My eyes were glued to the stage. My brother and I did not touch our phones throughout the summit unless we were on a break. That says a lot for us millennials. There were so many creative juices flowing through my brain. I was so motivated! It blew my mind that these entrepreneurs were selling from the stage and making millions by just sharing their stories and pouring knowledge into their audience.

These speakers were making millions using the instrument that I always got in trouble with in class. My teachers referred to me as "the social butterfly." I was never a behavioral problem; I just loved to talk. The bright idea came to me that I can do something I love and make money. This experience was just what I needed, being a recent college graduate. As soon as I got home, I brainstormed with my family, got some business cards and was ready to rock and roll. I know that I was made to inspire, motivate, and empower in whatever profession I take on; furthermore, I realized that I want to help people be their best selves through fashion, fitness, and faith. The new triple threat!

Having an answer to the question, "What do I want to do?" was a big "Yay" moment for me. The even bigger question was, "How am I going to promote my business in order to help the millions I desired to help?" After some thought, I knew that, in order to reach the masses of hearts and minds that I desired, being a good speaker had to be a quality of mine.

Once I knew that, I desired to find someone to help me perfect my craft. My speaking was decent enough to get by in school for a group project or two and for holding positions in organizations, but I desired to be better. Soon after, my mother introduced me to the Women's Prosperity Network's Speakers' Boot Camp that absolutely changed my life for the better. I am no longer afraid of losing my spot on my paper, because my speech is coming from the heart.

I gained clarity and more confidence in my speaking abilities. Now that I am a speaker, my confidence level has shot up while being on stage. I am sure of myself. It feels so amazing to have this clarity at this age, because I feel that the only way I can go is up!

Speaking has impacted me in such a phenomenal way. I'm able to connect with my audience and have them realize that they're not by themselves. I'm able to convey my story and feelings through my words, so my audience can truly connect with me. One thing that I enjoy is seeing the audience bright eyed and ready to receive the information that I'm about to give them. It makes my heart smile.

If you are considering taking your own journey to the stage, know that nobody connects with perfection. Be yourself and everything will blossom from there. My journey to the stage showed me that I want to help people "Be Uniquely and Completely You." What's your story?

"The only thing keeping you from your next level of success is the current level of your resistance." ~ Trish Carr

Angie LeBlanc is an Integrative Health Coach with an associate's degree in office administration from Nicholls State University. She enjoys working in her home office building a home-based business with Plexus Worldwide, a leader in the health and wellness industry that allows her to support business partners across the United States. The Louisiana-based entrepreneur is a member of the Houma-Terrebonne Chamber of Commerce, Women's Prosperity Network, Leadership Terrebonne Alumni Association and the American Business Women's Association.

You can contact Angie at info@angiebleblanc.com and www.angiebleblanc.com. You can also find her on Social Media: Facebook, Twitter, LinkedIn and Periscope.

The Accidental Entrepreneur . . . Now What?

Angie LeBlanc

Spending a lifetime working for someone else is the way it's supposed to be — at least that's what the resilient personalities responsible for my upbringing instilled in me. Go to school, get an education, find a job and be grateful for the little things. This simple way of life, growing up in a small Louisiana town, was all I had ever known.

Like many of my peers at a time when pursuing higher education was becoming more essential for life advancement, I pursued a college degree with the expectation to graduate and immediately seek employment. I started my life journey convinced that I was destined to be a teacher. That changed after I volunteered to teach a religion program for 7-year-olds. Suddenly, secretarial work became more enticing, so I began taking classes geared toward learning the many roles of administrative professionals. These classes were more enjoyable and felt like a natural fit — remember, whatever career I chose would be the career I would have to live with for the rest of my life ... so I had been convinced.

My first dose of reality came rather quickly. Odds are that you won't find *the* job for you the first time you fill out a W-4 form. My first opportunity found me leading an annual fundraising campaign for a nonprofit organization. The job required me to visit large companies and speak to employees about the services my nonprofit organization could offer. The idea was to have these employees commit to contributing money weekly so we could reach our annual goal. Such an aggressive assignment typically would be a nightmare for those like me who fear speaking in public, but the services benefited children. I kept reminding myself that I was on a mission to help those who were in no position to help themselves. My time at the nonprofit organization was short-lived due to the lack of a benefits package, which I needed, so my search continued for *that* lifetime job.

After adding several jobs to my growing résumé — and gaining lots of experience in the process — *the* job finally fell into my lap. Having taken an interest in technology's evolving role in the modern workforce, I landed an office manager position at a small oilfield supply company. My first task was to input all the manual bookwork — yep, green ledger sheets — into a computer system in order to track transactions for two locations. What was I thinking? Struggles popped up daily, but my sense of accomplishment was huge. My God-given organizational skills got the job done. I was working 8 to 5, Monday through Friday, off on weekends. Life was good.

There was just one problem: After working 13 years in such a robotic life pattern, I was bored.

Blessed with an entrepreneurial spirit, I dreamed of having the flexible schedule that comes with being one's own boss. But I never had the guts to follow through. I wasn't supposed to, said my resilient upbringing. The sun rose and the sun set, again and again, and with each passing day I asked myself two questions: What is my purpose in life? How can I bless people? I had a good life, but I yearned for more. Sound familiar?

Then a second dose of reality hit me: My lack of self-confidence and struggle with weight were keeping me from exploring alternatives that would give me a better life — and I was letting that happen. It's no secret that Louisiana cooks up the good stuff ... and not much about the good stuff is healthy. Those who grow up in my culture have a zest for life unlike any other community. Our traditions are planned around hearty flavors, festive music and endless fun.

Still stuck in my office manager position but now aware of what was holding me back, I was introduced to a product that had helped a friend on her weight loss journey. She assured me that this program was both easy to follow and affordable. Sold on giving it a try, I started the program and began to see results. I lost weight, felt better and had more energy. The program offered a business opportunity, but starting my own business still wasn't *really* on my radar. Family, friends and co-workers began noticing that I was dropping pounds and inquired about the source of my transformation. I explained the program to them. In no time, this newfound business that I had practically ignored began growing at a rate that forced me to take note. Success story after success story was being shared. Those around me were embracing a healthier lifestyle. What was I to do?

Right on time, my third dose of reality showed up: Follow your gut. Mine was screaming at me to jump into entrepreneurship. My passion became clear. I found myself removed from the past and resolute to carve a new path in my life. Ironically, my mother had been an entrepreneur for 50 years, despite the career expectations that had permeated my way of thinking as a young adult. I had forgotten this until she told me I was crazy for quitting my *perfect* job and taking a leap of faith.

The leap that I took seemed as giant as Neil Armstrong's back in 1969, but I understood that it would be up to me to make the most of it. I turned to industry experts and tutorials on video streaming websites like YouTube to learn more about the modern entrepreneur's essential steps for success. My organizational skills surfaced naturally. I began searching for systems that were already in place ... but I was my own boss now. It was my responsibility to create my own systems, or partner with a business coach to help me set a foundation. This strategy produced what has become a successful business, with the added benefit of a lifelong friendship.

Together, my business coach and I celebrate our successes, but she also challenges me to grow both as an entrepreneur and as a person. Aware of my public speaking fear, she pushed me to address this speed bump honestly and sign up to participate in speaking engagements. I didn't like this idea at all, but the reality is that such a fear has only one guaranteed remedy. I knew I would have to speak publicly if I was going to fulfill what was being revealed as my life's purpose — to inspire women to reach their full potential—so I signed up to speak.

Standing at a mic in front of a silent crowd is scary, even for the pros. Chatting with the audience before and after a presentation helps to rid the room of unspoken awkwardness. I met Mona, my business partner, during one of these chats. Mona sat in the back of the room but had an approachable demeanor, so I walked up, introduced myself and thanked her for taking the time to listen to what I had to say. I had no intention of ever seeing her again. Four years later, Mona and I still reminisce about the day we met. She had been sitting near the exit that day because, like me, she was terrified of speaking publicly. Not anymore. These days, Mona leads discussions and workshops on our products and business — front and center of the room.

Of all the speaking engagements I have hosted, one of my favorites remains a stop in Vermont. It was a trip of firsts for me: My first time in the Green Mountain State, my first time seeing a covered bridge, my first time flying solo, my first time speaking solo, my first time having baggage searched followed by the confiscation of a jar of peanut butter.

As for my most rewarding speech, it took place in Nebraska. My new business partner was in need of support to open a new market. She had put in many hours promoting her event and inviting guests. Speaking publicly was not a fear for her — she just needed a good example to break the ice and get the discussion started. The pressure was on, and I felt it. It was my responsibility to capture — and keep — the audience's attention while providing an example for my business partner to learn and follow. I nailed it, and today she is nailing it and prospering in her own community.

Entrepreneurship can be intimidating, especially when you grow up learning that being your own boss is a luxury reserved only for the privileged few. I have come to learn that this way of thinking is driven by the kind of fear that causes you to believe lies about yourself, thereby stunting personal growth. In addition, I have learned that challenging myself to overcome this fear and embrace the entrepreneurial spirit leads to worthwhile rewards, like being able to manage my own schedule so I can be with family and friends when they need me most.

Back in 2012, my mom was diagnosed with stage two breast cancer. She accepted the news like the strong woman she always has been. When Mom began chemotherapy treatments, I would join her as the nurses escorted us to a room filled with about 22 chairs, most of which were occupied. The stories I heard from the patients sitting in those chairs were heartbreaking. Some had been visiting the treatment center for years, spending hours at a time in that room. Mom's turn to ring the bell came in 2013, when she celebrated the end of her treatments. She is now cancer-free.

Looking back on Mom's recent journey toward becoming a healthier individual, I feel blessed to have had an *aha!* moment while accompanying her on a session at the cancer treatment center. "Why are so many people sick?" I asked myself. To learn the detailed answer to this question, I enrolled at the Institute for Integrative Nutrition with the intent to become a health coach. I knew this training would both educate me on the topic and allow me to gain a better understanding of how to support my clients on their journeys to improved health. As my studies advanced, I was rewarded with the proof I needed to be assured that my passion for supporting women's health and wellness is real. I once thought I had accidentally become an entrepreneur, but as my path and purpose become clearer, I now know that being my own boss is no accident.

"Where focus goes, energy flows." ~ Jake Merriman

Debra Melillo was promoted to Director of Planning and Development for Plan for Life, Inc., in four short months, having had no previous experience in the insurance or benefits consulting industries. Her background includes being an accomplished sales executive for companies like Berkshire Hathaway/The Marmon Group working with major retailers like TJX Companies, Publix, and Office Depot in the store fixtures and POP business. Additionally, she holds a Florida Real Estate Brokerage license, owning her own brokerage company for several years which included a real estate radio show. She studied Fashion Design and Merchandising at UCLA and currently resides on the Treasure Coast of Florida.

Debra will make herself available for guidance, support, chat at (772) 708-6922 or debramelillo@yahoo.com (Put Journey to the Stage in the subject line of your email)

You Are Power and Love

Dedicated to My loving Mother, Ersilia, Anna, Faith and Grace and Eddie Spaghetti

Debra Melillo

"You are not a victim; you are power and love." These are the words that came to me around 9:30pm January 9, 2015, in the final moments of my beloved stepfather's life. I believe he spoke them to me as he was making his journey from his physical presence to his eternal presence from his hospice bed. It was in this moment that a significant sense of peace, love and light filled my soul and calmed me for the first time in what seemed like an eternity.

My "Journey to the Stage" is literal and metaphorical as 2014 was a significantly transitional year in my life. Everything I knew that was constant changed in a very short span of time. My husband and best friend of 20 years moved out February 16, 2014. My stepfather, Eddie Spaghetti, General Curtis Lamay's hand-picked flight engineer during WWII, who had never been sick and was an amazing man was diagnosed with an Astrocytoma Brain Tumor on May 2, 2014 the same day I was downsized from my corporate American job as a sales executive. And if that wasn't enough, I started menopause. I felt lonely because seeing most of our friends felt like too painful a reminder of the life that had evaporated. I was left feeling empty, broken, depressed, anxious and lost. I could not sleep or eat. My weight plummeted to 102. Yes, I know, poor me. Trust me, it wasn't pretty! I was physically ill.

Fortunately, my loving mother was there for me. I also found myself surrounded by Faith, my neighbor, Grace, an old acquaintance who became a true friend, and my dearest friend, Anna. These ladies are my angels from God (It is ironic that two of them are named Faith and Grace!) who each contributed their own loving gifts to me when I needed them most, guiding me back toward finding myself and helping me heal. I am forever grateful!

In mid-December Grace introduced me to a neurologically trained chiropractor, Dr. Horne. He and his loving staff at Premier Wellness Centers helped restore my physical health, leading to the restoration of my mental health. I had tried several other medical methods with little success. I embraced whatever therapies he recommended and followed his instructions faithfully. I began to gain weight back, be able to sleep, and have the desire to get up in the morning, get dressed, and put on makeup and nice clothes. My lifestyle has always included maintaining a healthy diet and a having a love of exercising and doing yoga. I began to incorporate these activities back into my life, which I believe continues to perpetuate a positive cycle of mental and physical well-being.

As I was starting to re-bloom, I was invited to take a look at a career opportunity with Plan for Life, Inc., which is a business and benefits consulting company. My mother and I were Ed's Health Care Surrogates during his illness, managing his health care and the HUGE costs associated with his care not covered by Medicare or the VA. My role with Plan for Life would be to educate businesses and individuals on solutions for health care costs and avoiding having the financial burden of this scenario happen to them and their families. Plan for Life also educates consumers and businesses on creating tax-free income that could be used in these and other life situations, as well as providing strategies to build on and create new client/customer bases, retain and attract loyal employees and reduce costs associated with their everyday business dealings. Our "Dream Team" at Plan for Life is positive and supportive, making this the perfect fit for my transition, and I am thriving in my new career. I love helping people!

This position has required me to obtain the Florida 215 license, join networking groups and effectively articulate the value we bring to our clients. I joined the Chamber of Commerce and networking groups which provide me the opportunity to do 30-second business introduction speeches. Although I come from a corporate background and have given presentations for most of my 30-year career, I knew I could improve, so I joined a Friday-morning Talking Heads of Stuart Toastmasters Group.

After the first meeting, I was hooked! I have had other opportunities to work on public speaking, but this just felt right and is the most comfortable for me. Our group is lively, fun, smart and supportive. It has enabled me to learn public speaking technique and speech organization, gain confidence, learn how to effectively listen, make new friends, and set goals that will enhance my public speaking career. We have several members who are Distinguished Toastmasters and many members with much public speaking experience who are always available to guide, support and teach newer members how to move forward, effectively communicating and articulating their ideas. And we do this with a wicked sense of humor!

In mid-March, Dr. Horne invited me to a dinner Premier Wellness Center was hosting for new and existing patients. He asked if I would be willing to speak before a group of 50 or so people, sharing my health experience and how my recovery was impacted by their loving care. I was overjoyed, elated, and felt honored that their office team had that much confidence in me being able to deliver a message that might inspire others.

Members of my Toastmasters group helped guide me as I was preparing for my speech and joined me at the dinner. Additionally, colleagues from Plan for Life attended the dinner and were there holding positive space for me to thrive and succeed. It was an amazing experience that helped me gain the confidence to continue to pursue the dream of delivering a heartfelt message meant to positively inspire others to action toward their own success.

Currently, I find myself surrounded by a growing number of positive and open-minded friends and colleagues. My entire life has changed and while I am still adjusting to the fallout, I find the ground beneath my feet getting more solid with each passing day. I continue to pursue public speaking and have had other opportunities to speak on various topics that are near and dear to my heart, including environmental issues. I have found that the best messages I can deliver come from my heart, not my head. In fact, a friend recently said, "I have seen your heart run away with your head...." This is probably the nicest compliment a corporate American sales executive could receive—especially   one who thought working from her head was the best way to success but found that speaking and acting from the heart actually builds stronger character and provides some serenity.

I am love and power. That has become my mantra. I hope that these words will empower anyone reading them to reach for the greatness in their own heart. You are love and power!

Elin Mayer has been a motivational and incentive behavioral expert for over 30 years, speaking and teaching her Dream Builder programs with surprisingly effective results. With a degree in Theater and Public Speaking, she is in the "zone" when inspiring and having an impact on her students and audiences, both corporate and personal. She is a Certified Dream Builder Coach and Life Master Business and Personal Coach, conducting group and one-on-one coaching and curriculum-based strategies.

Check out her website at www.werockyourdream.com or email her for a complimentary half-hour life strategy session at elin@mayermotivations.com.

Puppets and Paradigms

Elin Mayer

Shirley Temple and Puppets Started the Dream

It was the Shirley Temple era for little girls, bouncy curls and cute, cute, cute till you gritted your teeth on sweetness. And my Mom turned me into a little Shirley Temple at 2 years old and taught me to say this (complete with hand motions if you want to learn it):

> *Big Blue Eyes (fingers open wide on the outside of each eye)*
> *Oh, what a figure! (hands on hips)*
> *Get away, boys, (push both hands out in front of you to stop those boys)*
> *Just wait till I'm bigger! (both hands back on hips and shimmy)*

Family and friends thought this was just too adorable, and lawdy, lawdy, I received applause! It was like M&M's to a chocoholic. I gobbled up the laughter and fun I created for my fan club – and repeated my act over and over again to the same tireless audiences.

Little 2-year olds are impressionable, both in positive and negative ways. And for that little "me" – Wow! – was that a positive impression that got processed in my conscious mind and then got buried deep in my subconscious.

Now I don't want you to think I was so positively impressed that I wore Shirley Temple curls and Mary Jane shoes for the rest of my life, but a vivid dream was born and from two years old and onward, I had a "yearn and burn" to perform and impact audiences—to inspire them, amuse them, and take them away from their troubles, just for a time.

I made a big step in the direction of my dream when I was 4 years old with a full-blown hand puppet show live sitcom that involved a fox, a bear and a dog. I performed behind a classy puppet stage made of painted cardboard boxes decorated by my Dad with genuine red velvet stage curtains!

This was a fantasy – a dream come true – on a journey to the stage!

I became the showbiz hit of the "little girls' 6-10-year-old birthday party circuit" and was even paid by a couple of adult groups to perform. At the adult parties I made $2 – double what I got paid at the little girl parties. I was a professional at 4 and was already taking steps toward achieving my dream of speaking and performing.

More Fantasies

Of course there were more fantasies, more dreams, and some of them scared me. That's what it looks like on your journey to the stage. Scary. At 17 I fantasized about writing a musical play for the Kansas Centennial Celebration and, wow, was I terrified. Yet I kept the vision in mind, didn't listen to my paradigms (What are those? More later...) and wrote and directed a production like no other, with 27 actors, the full school orchestra and the choral group. I went on TV, was written up in newspapers throughout the region and stayed terrified through the whole thing. It was the fantasy, the end game that got me through, in spite of those pesky paradigms.

What in the Heck is a Paradigm?

Ok, so you're fantasizing about your dream and ultimate success – whether a beginning speaker or one that wants higher-paid gigs! All of a sudden, doubting thoughts and voices that are a collection of beliefs (usually from your past) interrupt your fun. Doubting voices say things like, *"What do you mean you want to be a speaker or have bigger audiences or get paid more? WHAT?? Who do you think you are? What if the audience doesn't like you? That's too much money to ask! You'll fail. You don't have what it takes. You're too old, too fat, too skinny, to curvy, too pretty, too ugly, wear too many polka dots... Stop this useless dreaming!! Just sit yourself down with me where you belong – in your limited thinking— and stay here with me in your big recliner of a comfort zone!!*

And then, just like a deflated balloon, your goal and vision collapse.

A Strong Specific Fantasy or Dream

Yes, a strong specific fantasy or dream...keeps your balloon inflated. Paradigms (just like the puppet shows I used to have) are hand-manipulated by your mind to stop you from going to the edge of the life you have known up until now.

If your dream is strong and specific, heavenly obliviousness to the voices of your Christmases Past, or any past, sets in your mind, and you only see the vision and the dream. The voices of doubt get tuned out – you've changed the channel and the frequency. Be gone!! And they are!

How do you make your dream strong enough to do this? As a Dream Builder coach, I can't give you all the skills in a 1500-word chapter, yet you can learn them, as they are specific and repeatable. One tip: Take 10 minutes a day to create a movie for yourself in your mind. Make it full color and fun like a Pixar production. Make this movie as if it were happening now. Where are you? How many in the audience? What's your subject? How much are you getting paid? Imagine!! Imagine!!

Here's what a guy named Einstein had to say about imagining: *"Imagination is more important than knowledge. For knowledge is limited to all we now know and understand, while imagination embraces all there ever will be to know and understand."*

Here we go, another tip: Be specific with your fantasy. If you're not specific in your dream, you can end up getting something you really didn't want. Would you pick up the phone, call Macy's and say to the operator, "Hi, here is my name and address and credit card – just send me something you think I'd like…."

That's like wanting to speak passionately for a fundraiser about "Helping Disadvantaged Children" and you are offered a booking at a very high price (oh, exciting!) yet discover the night you are to go on stage that the client wants a three-hour workshop on the " New Techniques of Breeding Goats" – guess what? You have just called Macy's and asked for, well, you know…whatever they thought you might like. Horrible moment!! (Not that populating the world with more goats isn't important....)

What helped me on my journey to the stage was the strong desire I have had since I was 2 years old to speak and perform. You can be 85 and create this strong desire – you just need to learn the specific skills and follow them. You can activate <u>now</u> any dream you want. Whether you are just starting out or are a speaker now, you can fantasize yourself to fame and fortune through developing a strong specific dream that will prevent the naysayers of your mind (and also outside your mind) from stomping their foot and insisting you stay in your comfort zone!

The minute those "voices of doubt, fear, worry, disapproval, ja da, ja da" interrupt, hold the horses, stop the train, step on the brake and immediately jump into that fantasy right away. Imagine your dream, visualize and, by the way, think how you would feel during your speech. Magic, maybe?

And how do you feel during the applause? Oh, don't we love that! Imagine what an impact you have made on the audience by speaking about "Helping Disadvantaged Children" and the funds you have raised for this important cause. You've been specific about what you want, and you won't have the "Breeding Goats" shock to deal with.

When I finally designed a dream, I fantasized a slim and skinny me wearing a red suit, and red shoes, standing on a stage and experiencing the high of all high's—a standing ovation from 5,000 people. It made me cry, it made me laugh, it made me giggle. And I return to that imagined vision every time I hear a voice of doubt. I haven't got the red suit yet and standing ovations from 5,000 are on the way, but I did lose 100 pounds and have red shoes – from visualizing and imagining the end game and how it feels.

Fantasize Your Way to Success

Visualize the end game in living color. And then magic happens – the magic of learning the right actions to achieve this fantasy fearlessly – you'll symbolically take your hearing aid out when you hear a voice of fear and doubt and jolt yourself right back into that fantasy. And you will have a sudden "feeling good" moment. Delicious!! And that puts you in the same vibration as your dream.

There is so much more to tell you – this is just the introduction to the whole splendid plan!! But I leave you with a success code found in a quote by Henry David Thoreau, the "CODE" is in italics – and it works!! That's how I got to the stage as a happy paid speaker!! "I learned this, at least, by my experiment: that *if one advances confidently in the direction of his dreams, and endeavors to live the life which he has imagined, he will meet with a success_unexpected in common hours.*"

If you have built castles in the air, your work need not be lost; that is where they should be. Now put the foundations under them.

1. Advance confidently in the direction of your dream (Ya gotta have a dream)

2. Endeavor to live the life which you have imagined (Ya gotta have a dream)

3. You will be successful (Your dream will come true)

4. You have built castles in the air(Ya gotta have a dream)

5. Now put the foundations under them (You can learn to do this with a mentor)

Ellen McDowell is the founder of Ellen McDowell – Your Social Butterfly. She is a Master Certified Constant Contact Solution Provider and Authorized Local Expert for Constant Contact, Board member of the LaCapitale Chapter ABWA, a Certified Professional Speaker, and proud Chapter Co-Leader for the Baton Rouge Women's Prosperity Network. She speaks regionally to small business owners and entrepreneurs on best practices for incorporating email and social media marketing. She is an oenophile and avid LSU Superfan – GEAUX Tigers!

You can set a phone call or meeting with Ellen online at www.ellenmcdowell.com. You can also find her on Facebook, LinkedIn, Twitter, Google+, Instagram, and YouTube.

On Stage Again, Without My Dancing Shoes

Ellen McDowell

I hope you are reading this book because you're preparing for your own journey to a stage. It's such a fulfilling undertaking!

My own journey to the stage is more my journey *back* to the stage. Throughout my life, I have performed on various stages and in front of different audiences. From high school dance and drama to speaking to professional organizations, my life has been preparing me to get on a stage and present something to others. I hope I can help you realize that, because of your life experiences, you are more prepared than you might think.

One of my first ventures onto a stage came at a fairly young age. Like most young girls in the south, I took dance lessons. We had a yearly recital presenting the ballet, tap, and jazz routines we had practiced all year, and by the time I was in high school, I danced solos. I look back on this stage experience with not only fond memories but also the knowledge that it gave a shy young teen more confidence and composure to go on stage in front of a large audience.

I am not sure I ever believed I was good enough to be a soloist. Years later, though, I met someone at a party who told me how much she had enjoyed watching my dances when she was one of the younger girls at the dance school. I was shocked that anyone even remembered me, much less thought I was talented!

Many people get some stage experience with high school drama courses. I did take drama and enjoyed it, but I was always backstage during the productions. This was not necessarily by choice; I remember trying out for a few parts and being jealous of the actors who got them. I think the drama teacher knew that I was good at details and would get done the tasks necessary to having a successful stage production, so I was assigned backstage roles. I find it hard even years later to give up the backstage preparations for seminars.

Remember when you are preparing to give your presentations, you can and should get help to prepare ahead of time and after the event is over. Surround yourself with a good team to enhance your talents, because we're all better with a support team in place.

My college years also included preparation for speaking to an audience, but to smaller groups. My bachelor's degree is in interior design and my college emphasized presenting semester projects to groups. Having to defend a project to peers and visiting professionals was nerve wracking. The instructors and professionals were there to point out all the details that were not quite right with what I'd spent weeks and many late nights finalizing. Presenting under pressure, and on just a couple of catnaps grabbed in the last two weeks of the semester, made for a special kind of stress that speaking to groups will never replicate (at least that is my hope for you!).

If you asked if my career as a designer gave me any preparation to get on a stage, I would probably tell you, "Of course not! I only spoke to my clients!" But then if I think a little more on that, presenting design ideas to a client is a speaking engagement itself. Presenting how beautiful a room is going to be and how it meets all of the needs discussed is planned and practiced just like any other speech. Even if you only present your ideas to a couple of your work teammates, that's also preparing you for speaking.

I live in the same town as the University from which I graduated, so when I had the opportunity to teach there in an adjunct role, I jumped at the chance. I think back now on preparing to walk into the large lecture hall to present *Introduction to Interior Design* to a group composed primarily of freshmen, and I am thankful that almost all of the lectures were prepared and given to me by the lead professor!

ID1051 is a course that is popular because many students sign up thinking that it will be "an easy A". It is not. I think the only thing that got me through the teaching experience is that I loved sharing information about my profession, and at that point, I knew more than they did. (That thought still gets me through most of my presentations!)

I spend time learning more about the subject on which I am presenting to make sure that I know more than my audience knows on the topic. You know more than most people in your audience; remember, the simple fact that you're at the front of the room makes you the expert!

Like many professionals, I've joined a number of professional organizations throughout my career. My problem is I never just join and attend the meetings merely to enjoy the benefits of membership. I volunteer for committees and quickly move into leadership positions.

I've realized that leading committee meetings or the monthly meetings of the organization is another preparation for speaking engagements. After all, I am presenting my ideas of how to run the committee's work, or leading a meeting so it runs on time and is relevant to the topic at hand. If you are a member of a professional organization, join a committee or two. The group you belong to needs your help, and being in a leadership role will give you the opportunity to speak to a small group when you give your reports. It's a small and natural way of easing yourself into speaking in front of others.

Why do I now choose to get on an actual stage? The short answer is that I love to help people (especially small business owners) with social media and email marketing. When I was laid off from an online university a few years ago, my mother encouraged me to find a way to keep teaching and utilize my natural ability to share knowledge.

I've never had a desire to teach in a setting that required publishing to keep the job. Yet here I am embarking on a career as an author! Each of us has to find both the message and the medium that's right for us.

The best way I have found for me to share my expertise is to present in person to larger groups of entrepreneurs and small business owners. I have to put aside any fear or thoughts that what I have to share isn't unique. I wrote a blog post recently, reflecting on how, no matter how many times I think I have heard something, there is always someone out there who is hearing it for the very first time. And many people need to hear something repeated three or more times before it's really grasped.

I give out good information that helps people

communicate with their clients more effectively. While the presentations I give seem very basic to some, I share information that many new entrepreneurs find overwhelming. Many of the people who attend leave feeling like they've learned social media or email marketing ideas that they can apply to their own situations.

I am always humbled when I review the evaluation forms from my audience. (Tip: if you are not collecting contact information at the time of event registration, collect it during your presentation!) It is so satisfying at the end of an event to know that I have assisted others to do better. It is also exhausting work; it amazes me how I feel both drained and exhilarated when I arrive home after speaking.

As I look back now, I realize that all of my life experiences have prepared me to step out of my comfort zone and walk out on stage to share my knowledge with others. Reflect on your own past; I suspect that you will find a few similar experiences that could be equipping you to step out on stage too.

Our personal histories prepare us all for our futures. Whether you're wearing dancing shoes or not, I wish you the best as your own curtain rises!

Catherine M. Laub is an Angel Communication Master helping clients decipher their lives to plan better futures. Catherine has work forthcoming in two books. In *Chocolate & Diamonds for the Woman's Soul,* she talks about her healing journey. Book 4 of *The Inner Circle Chronicles* with Anne Deidre is about spirituality and personal challenges. She is married to Tony, and has 7 children and 13 grandchildren, Joshua being her closest because he loves to visit with Gma. Catherine's angels just gave her a new mission to speak about depression.

You can learn more about Catherine at
www.catherinemlaub.com.

My Journey to the Stage

Catherine M. Laub

I recently wrote about *My Healing Journey* in *Chocolate & Diamonds for the Woman's Soul*. I spoke of my most debilitating illnesses and overcoming them. Here I elaborate a little more because my healing is what brought me to the stage.

My "living in the bathroom" was not fun or comfortable. I would have to run and just make it and other times had accidents. I spent so much time "sitting" that Tony (my husband) built me a drop down shelf in our small bathroom. I did a lot of reading and word puzzles in there. I didn't sleep well because I was getting up many times and couldn't fall back to sleep. I always told people my disposal system didn't work well. It sounds funny but really was very stressful. This is where my mind and body work together and my poor health caused my depression to be terrible and vice versa. I trust my angels to protect me from needing any more surgeries. I had so many I felt like the hospital had a revolving door.

It is tough living with depression and anxiety. It is a feeling of being stuck and having no direction in life. I never wanted or was capable of doing much physically so I mostly watched TV daily. Tony shopped, cooked and cleaned. He also took care of me.

Since my suicide attempt last August, I have been on the right path. I found new doctors who made changes in my medications. In April I met Dr. David Pollack, a holistic practitioner in Commack, New York. He has been treating me specific to my symptoms, and I am eating an organic diet which lessens my inflammation. Within two weeks I was amazed at the changes in my health. Until then I would be afraid to leave my house due to needing a bathroom in an emergency. I am now managing to leave my house once a week for my doctor visits, and I'm attending classes and business meetings at least once a week. I am not cured but am able to make plans without many worries.

I was on a spiritual path all my life but nothing ever came together like it does now. Since I began my angel communication classes, my angels told me to do readings for income. So I followed their direction and became an angel communication master. This was after joining the class in September, 2011, having a nervous breakdown that December, and having to put the class on hold. Again September, 2012, I was set to join the class, but my teacher Reverend Elvia suggested I wait because I was to have major surgery in October. So, finally in 2013, I took my course and received my certification.

I worked for Tony from 2001 to 2013 as his office manager/bookkeeper. After my last surgery I couldn't work. I was on temporary disability and when it was time to "return to work", Tony was closing the company and we filed for bankruptcy. I hadn't been working much anyway because of my depression and there being not much work for me to do. The little I did was from home.

I began my business while unemployed through a

government program which allowed me to continue receiving full benefits. I put a lot of money, time and effort into it but to no avail. I prayed it would work because I could not work for an employer. With my poor health, I wasn't reliable. My attempt at business in 2013 lasted five months until my unemployment benefits ended, and I didn't have any more funds to invest. That is when I applied for Social Security disability. We struggled to make ends meet because we lived on Tony's Social Security income. I was denied the first time and was finally approved, based on my appeal, in January, 2015.

I am attending coaching classes in person, online and on the telephone. I am still on my journey but learned to put programs together to offer my clients more than just an angel reading. I learned my negative experiences were necessary for me to be able to share. I can offer solace to my clients that things can get better. I offer compassion because I know what they are going through.

While talking with my therapist, Patricia Firestone of Holbrook Learning Center in New York, we discovered that I open doors for people by sharing my story. I help them realize there is so much more to life and it's possible to achieve anything we reach for.

Through my coaching program with Women's Prosperity Network, I learned I am talking to the wrong audience. I was guided to join local meet-up groups. Most of them are to advance my skills to add Mediumship, and I am making connections to do readings at psychic fairs.

While at a craft fair, I met a local psychic and was invited to talk on her TV show. I discussed my skills and healing journey and she was intrigued. I described a new campaign my angels want me to work on. They want me to speak about depression. They gave me a slogan and directions to spread the word that it is OK to acknowledge being depressed. By doing so, it is an opening to get the guidance needed to feel better. The slogan I was given is: "Brighten your day with turquoise."

Being depressed is very stressful. People are afraid to admit it because they don't want others to think badly of them. The fact is, with all the turmoil in the world today, a lot more people are becoming depressed. There is so much unemployment in the United States, which can cause a domino effect in our lives. A big issue is people losing their homes and some ending up homeless. This causes people to feel like nothing will ever get better. I am here to tell you that it can!

I suffered from depression for as long as I can remember. The first big "episode" was in 1992 when my husband left me. I was in such bad shape the first few months I couldn't fully care for my three young children without help from my parents. I used to sit on the edge of my bed and just stare into space. My therapist at the time told my mother to watch over me because I could snap. I lived with my parents and eventually had a fight with my mother. I felt up against a wall with nowhere to turn, and I wanted a new place to live. I wrote, "If I was going to commit suicide, it would be tonight." I was prescribed an antidepressant, and now realize I should have discussed further treatment. I met Tony during that time and he let us move to a rental home he owned. I managed to attend BOCES, a technical school for office technology and computer classes, while I was caring for my children alone.

Through the years I didn't realize I was still depressed. In 2003 there was a lot going on with Tony's business and various other situations, and we fought a lot. I snapped while at the office. I left and drove to my parents' home so my mother could take me to be admitted to the hospital. I was hospitalized for a week and learned a lot of coping skills. For six weeks, I went to an outpatient hospital until I was feeling better. In 2011 I fell apart again and was hospitalized for a week and then went to the outpatient program again. There was even the Tuesday before Thanksgiving one year that, while at my psychiatrist's office, I was suicidal and there were no available hospital beds. The doctor sent me home and told my friend to babysit me till I felt better.

I feel confident in saying my last hospitalization was my last because my angels have brought me through the worst of my depression. The biggest thing I learned, even though I already knew it, was to "put the oxygen mask on myself first". I had to stop helping everyone else and take care of myself. With the help of Dr. Pollack and Patricia Firestone, as mentioned above, I am doing so and feel much better.

As I write this, I am thinking about my next adventure. In October I will go to Santa Barbara, California, to meet with 12 people who are collaborating on another book. It will be book 4 in a series of *The Inner Circle Chronicles*. Men and women will share their wisdom and insights about the new economy and shift that is happening now on this planet. If I hadn't been on this healing journey, I would never have thought to go on such a long trip.

Melissa Binkley is CEO and Founder of MSB Wellness and Pure BodyLove Events. She is a **Certified Master Transformation Specialist** and **Holistic Health Coach**, and a dynamic **Inspirational Speaker**. She is the master of magic mindset, soul guided living and bodylove. She empowers women to break through limiting self-beliefs, *Perfectionist Paralysis* **and love their bodies, businesses and lives.** Known for her ability to transcend limiting beliefs, she uses techniques that fuse science, whole brain learning, personal development, and the quantum field. Melissa is a graduate of The Ohio State University, The Institute for Integrative Nutrition, and has a Holistic MBA. Her website was ranked one of the top 50 Health Coach Sites for 2013 by the Institute for Psychology of Eating. She has been featured nationwide on several radio shows and is a WEGO Health Activist Nominee and Runner-up.

Contact Melissa at Melissa@MelissaBinkley.com or www.MelissaBinkley.com.

Metamorphosis

Melissa Binkley

I was standing in front of 20 of my peers, getting ready to debate and speak about a secluded rare topic. I was only 17 and only three months away from the most tragic moment of my life—more tragic than losing my mother at nine, more tragic than being physically abused by my father, more tragic than being molested at ten. I was sweating streams down my back and could feel everyone's eyes locked on me. My opening statement, "One out of every four women in America will be sexually assaulted or raped in their lifetime. Look to your left, your right, and in front and behind you; who will be next if we don't change how society views sexuality, women, and the growing rape culture?"

I stood there as the one that had endured a brutal rape. I had endured the whispers, the comments from my classmates and other students. As I took my stand in front of this small group in my senior English class, my classmates sat with eyes wide and in hushed silence. I could only imagine their thoughts as I laid bare my soul as I presented my report on Rape Culture in America.

I had no idea in that moment that I was destined to share my life and stories on many stages, and that I would create a life, love, and business teaching people on every continent how to overcome their own challenges. I could feel the sweat trickle in lines like ants marching down my spine. My heart raced harder than when I would sprint 200 yards during a track meet. I felt raw and exposed. But this experience was the foundation I would use to build a business empire dedicated to helping women heal their lives, bodies, and minds.

The following May, I was asked to speak at our graduation ceremony as Salutatorian of the graduating class of 1995. I stood in my silky cap and gown, awkward and alone. I brought a room full of parents, grandparents, teachers, and students to tears with my engaging speech about life and moving forward. I couldn't control my emotions and tears streamed down my face—I believed this moment would heal my pain. It did not. It would be more than 15 years before I would risk being in front of audience again, seeing these experiences as a gift to share.

RISK—the definitive word for my journey to the stage. I spent the next ten years struggling through eating and exercise disorders, drug abuse, and body image issues. On the outside, my world appeared perfect—it seemed I had it all together—but on the inside I was slowly being eaten away. I had hidden all my hurt by burying it deep within myself

In 2009, I hit rock bottom. I've since learned that, before every breakthrough, there is a breakdown; you must break down old beliefs, ideas, and patterns so you can break through the pain to a new existence. I experienced the breakdown in every area of my life. First, I found a white slip of paper on my condo's door—I had three days to move—I had been evicted. Within a six-month time frame, I would be fired from my job, left by my girlfriend for another woman who was a close friend, *and* evicted from my apartment. I was heartbroken, homeless, and *very* unhappy. I felt betrayed, unloved, and lost. My beautiful daughter would be turning eleven soon. I knew it was past time for a big change.

I had felt the breakdown coming on for several years. When you consciously decide that it's time to heal your life, your whole world shifts and the universe conspires to bring you the answers you seek. Standing there that day at the lowest point in my adult life, I didn't know what the next step was, but I decided to open my heart, my ears, and my mind to listen for the answers. That was a defining moment for me, and one that would change my life forever. RISK—every opportunity, every choice, for the next few years would be a risk. I decided to become an entrepreneur for the second time in my life, and this business would be based on helping people. My desire to help others was the true path to finding out how to heal my own life and mind, and to *truly* make a change for the better. I quickly learned you can only help others once you've first helped yourself. This was the lesson for that part of my journey.

Since I had spent the last few years competing in the fitness world, I immediately went back into fitness training, thinking this was the way to serve others. But I still felt unfulfilled, and I wasn't enjoying the process of personal training. I instinctively knew that there was something greater to be discovered. I began reading personal development books, I reconnected with my spirituality, and I started practicing yoga. I learned about meditation, and I began to hear, feel, and know the secrets to creating a life I loved and a business that would thrive, while helping women worldwide transform their lives. I started opening up. I listened to the whispers of my heart. I began connecting to who I authentically am and listening to my gut and intuition.

Then the opportunities started showing up and my voice came back. I had always been a leader, a risk taker, the one to push the envelope and question everything, and I began using those qualities to move my life forward in a healthier and happier way.

By tapping into the universe, I was led to the Institute for Integrative Nutrition. This program started my journey and eventually led me to Holistic MBA to study Transformation Coaching. I studied many programs in order to deepen my knowledge, intuition, and spiritual wisdom. In 2001, I took to the stage after a 15-year hiatus. I began with small crowds of 1 to 20. In the beginning, I only spoke about health topics. I was fearful to share my story. But I soon I discovered it was my story that made me powerful, and once I decided to authentically start sharing my challenges, I discovered my challenges were solutions for other people.

In March of 2014, I took another big risk. I decided to host my first conference—The Pure BodyLove Retreat. That October, I gathered 15 speakers, healers, doctors, and scientists to share emotional, physical, and psychological transformation with nearly 150 people. I spent two entire days on stage training, speaking, and playing. I poured my heart, soul, and funds into creating this event. When it ended, I was forced into self-evaluation. The event had been successful; I made great connections, gained new clients and inspired women like I wanted. However, monetarily I came out negatively, which made me question the success of my event. In the end, I realized that even though I had come out in the red financially, I came out positively because of the impact I had made on the attendees of the event. I am know doing annual large retreats, conferences and events, sharing the stage with incredible, talent people from around the globe and my life has completely shifted.

I now travel the United States speaking at conferences and events, I have been a featured speaker on worldwide telesummits, and I've shared the stage with amazing, transformational leaders such as Dr. John Demartini. I'm currently planning my TEDx talk. My business has tripled for two years in a row, and in 2016 I am going international. My journey to the stage has changed my life and business, and touched the lives of women worldwide. I have built a team and looking to expand with more in the near future. My goal is to reach 1 billion people through my programs, speaking, books and foundation. I want a reach beyond my lifetime and a legacy that lives forever.

I offer Soulistic* solutions for women. I take women on a journey that feels like shamanism combined with past-life regression, infused with modern psychology and science. I'm the master of the magic mindset, soul guided living, and BodyLove! I love inspiring women to love the bodies they're in and breakthrough perfectionist paralysis and procrastination. I thrive on helping others create the health, wealth, and life they desire by overcoming their past and limiting self-beliefs using techniques that are spiritually based such as with quantum field work and holistic health. I am a Certified Master Transformation Specialist. I am Melissa Binkley.

Howard "Lucky" Luckman, The Information Alchemist, has spent the past 40+ years as a pioneer and visionary in the evolving information age. As a consultant, executive, writer and speaker, he has shared his understanding of how businesses can create and monetize their online presence. As an award-winning speaker with a Toastmasters Competent Communicator certification, he has spoken in front of groups from a few to hundreds on subjects ranging from technology to spirituality. He has spoken on and moderated technology and music industry panels and has been a featured speaker sharing the stage with some of America's best known technology leaders and spiritual advisors.

You can contact Howard at
Howard@theinformationalchemist.com
or (571) 716-4112.

The 3 P's to a Powerful Presentation

Howard "Lucky" Luckman

When it comes to public speaking, I have an advantage over most people. I grew up in New York City. As you may know, if there's one thing that New Yorkers enjoy more than a great slice of pizza, it's flapping our jaws.

Early Days

It didn't matter to me that I had no training about how to communicate. Whether in school, in social situations or at business meetings, I was always willing speak my mind. I just had confidence that I could deliver a message in a way that made sense to me. I didn't care if my audience could follow what I was saying, and if they didn't, well, like a typical New Yorker, I felt it was their loss.

Of course everything was not as rosy as it may sound. I often suffered from the dreaded foot-in-mouth disease when I would speak without thinking or without a clear message. Then one day I decided to record and listen to my own voice. When I turned the tape recorder to play, I broke out in a sweat hearing this nasal sounding New York accent coming out of the speaker. My inner critic jumped for joy and kept telling me how awful my voice was and no one would want to hear me speak.

Toastmasters

Then I caught a break. While I was living in Santa Monica in the 1980's, my acupuncturist suggested I join his Toastmasters group. I had always thought of Toastmasters as a group of old fogies giving totally boring speeches on subject matters that I couldn't care less about. Fortunately he convinced me it was a well varied group with inspiring speeches and talented speakers. It turned out it was an environment I would enjoy, in which I would learn new skills and hone my speaking techniques.

As I got ready to give my first Toastmasters speech, I was feeling very anxious. The thought of getting up in front of the group didn't bother me as much as my inner critic telling me my subject matter was boring, I would look foolish and my voice was not very pleasing. Then there was the fear of feedback I would be getting at the end of my speech that would criticize every aspect of my presentation.

Much to my surprise, I received the most amazing and supportive feedback. Every one of the club members, from novices to professional speakers to television and movie industry executives, told me what a fabulous voice I had and how I was able to deliver my message in a clear, concise and entertaining manner.

Decision Time

At that point I had a choice to make. Was I going to listen to my old friend, my critical inner voice, or was I going to listen to those who know what makes a good speaker?

Fortunately for me I chose to listen to those who know and told my inner critic to be quiet and accept the fact that I actually had a good voice and a strong presence to be an excellent speaker.

After giving several speeches and learning a variety of techniques on how to present my message, I was ready to try my hand at speaking to larger audiences and in sales environments. I started to speak at industry events as either a keynote speaker, panel member or moderator. I spoke about technology to groups ranging from a few to a few thousand and utilized my skills during sales presentations.

Applause for a Sales Presentation

One of my favorite stories is about the time I was selling email services (it was the early days of email and people and companies actually paid for email based on the size of the message). I gave a presentation to the Pepperdine University MBA students. The audience was made up of around 25-30 mid and upper level management types from the aerospace, financial and entertainment sectors. I was able to educate a very intelligent group on how the future held waves of electronic communications and email was the next wave. At the end of my sales presentation, I received a standing ovation and signed up several large accounts.

How? The 3 P's to a Powerful Presentation

How did I accomplish this type of success as a speaker and presenter? I learned the 3 P's of a powerful presentation: Preparation, Practice and Poise.

1. Preparation

I don't want to "P" on you too much, but I love acronyms and one of my favorites I learned from Prem Rawat (Search YouTube.com to see one dynamic speaker). He taught me to remember the 7 P's to Proper Preparation – Proper Prior Planning Prevents Piss Poor Performance. Before doing a planned speech or sales presentation, I would research my subject matter. Even if I thought I knew it all, I found by researching I could learn new and important information to include in my speeches.

I would then create a color coded mind map (see www.thebrain.com for information on mind maps and to download a free mind mapping tool) based on the key elements of my upcoming speech. I found I could give a 30-minute presentation from a good mind map drawn on a 3"x5" index card. In addition, the better prepared I was, the more confidence I would have that I would deliver a great presentation.

2. Practice

Hillary Clinton said, "If you're not comfortable with public speaking – and nobody starts out comfortable; you have to learn how to be comfortable – practice. I cannot overstate the importance of practicing."

Whenever I was going to give a prepared speech, I would stand in front of my mirror and practice, practice, practice. I would follow the different color coded options I built into my mind maps in case the audience was receptive to one train of thought more than another. I would try different body movements, facial expressions and voices until I felt I not only knew my material, but I could share what I knew in a way that my audience would be informed and entertained.

3. Poise

Poise is defined as "a dignified, self-confident manner or bearing." When speaking to a single person or a large group, poise helps give you the confidence to deliver your message in a way that it will be received by your audience. It is important that you have a good presence and dress appropriately for the environment in which you are speaking.

One of the things I do right before I give my speech is to get a picture of myself in my mind's eye. In my picture I make myself larger than life and insert streams of light coming out of me. This adds to my confidence and poise as I take the stage, and it is something that the audience picks up on. Try it the next time you are giving a speech. You will feel doubts dissipate and a subtle, strong sense of confidence that your audience will sense.

Feel confident that, even when the unexpected occurs, and it will, you know you have the ability and preparation to utilize any circumstance to your advantage. Make a joke or just go with the flow of the audience. When you are prepared, any challenge you face will be easy for you to handle.

The Exception to the Rule

Of course there is a major exception to the above formula.

That's when you have an opportunity to just speak from your heart. While the technique of making sure the self-image is large and glowing with light overcomes most of the vulnerability you may feel, when speaking in an impromptu format, just enjoy yourself, be yourself and share yourself. If you're true to yourself, you'll be a huge success.

Now You Are a Speaker

Now you have it, my formula to be a successful speaker. ***Yes, you***! I've seen totally shy people transform into dynamic speakers, and I've seen natural born talkers (many of whom are actually not from New York) hone their sales and speaking skills. Both have been able to enjoy the experience of being in front of a group of people, sharing a message that serves their audience and seeing the lights go on as the communication is established between speaker and audience. Just remember the 3 P's - Preparation, Practice and Poise, and you will know your subject, know your speech and know yourself. You'll actually look forward to giving speeches, sharing your knowledge with an engaged audience and reaping the benefits of being a powerful presenter.

"Vision is driven by action and without action, the vision will die. Taking action, even small steps, ensures your vision will live and come into being." ~ Nancy Matthews

Adele Alexandre is an award-winning Speaker, Storyteller and Professional Clown. She is a Teaching and Performing Artist and works in Dade, Broward, and Palm Beach Counties (FL) and in New England. For International Clown Week, held in August each year, she produces events for children's charities and performs along with her Joeys in the Krackerjak Clown Alley. She is featured in the YouTube video "Clowns of Coconut Creek." Adele is past President of the Palm Beach County Storytelling Guild, served on the Florida Storytelling Association Board, and mentors for Florida Storytelling Association's Youthful Voices (ages 8-18). She is a member of Toastmasters International, and is a sought-after workshop and conference leader, having won numerous awards in speaking contests.

Adele can be reached at MzMirtha@gmail.com, www.MzMirthasMerritown.com or (954)732-4356, talk or text.

Spotlight, Like Sunshine, Relaxes Me

Adele Alexandre

I have a clear memory of being a stuttering speaker. I stood in front of the attentive audience. There was no lectern for my handwritten notes. My hand shook so hard I could barely read my own handwriting as I shared my Icebreaker Speech, four to six minutes about myself. Adding to my nerves, the speech was being taped.

When I look back on this experience, I remember my mentors and teachers. At Rhode Island College, Professor Phillip Joyce encouraged me to join the Debate and Theater Clubs. I forced myself out of my shyness to attend these clubs, winning a Debate Club Scholarship, making and repairing costumes, and eventually was brave enough to appear in supporting roles, on stage, in several live theater productions.

I didn't love Debate Club. There was one topic all year long–the Vietnam War. I didn't love being on stage. I feared being in the wrong place at the wrong time, and I had a memory that was good, but way too short for leading roles.

In Florida, I attended an event where nationally known Storyteller Odds Bodkin told one story for a whole hour! I joined the Palm Beach County Storytelling Guild mailing list that day. At the Guild meetings I met Dr. Caren Neille, the Guild's founder and first President, and Mij Byram, the second President. Caren and Mij were my mentors and taught me about the Art of Storytelling. I do love Storytelling! This is something that I know and I can remember! I became the Guild's third President, and I administer its Face Book Page.

Storytelling in small groups is like sitting around your living room sharing experiences with your friends! No microphone and no reading are required as this is an oral art form. I discovered the Florida Storytelling Association, received a scholarship to Story Camp and was hooked! I was on the Board for two years and annually work with Youthful Voices, storytelling for children 8-18, as a mentor and play coach.

As a Nurse Midwife and Nurse Practitioner, I had spoken to audiences about Family Health Care. However, these talks were based on my experience, and I did not use or need notes. Writing speeches for Toastmasters was very difficult for me. Luckily, again, a mentor, Jeff Tockman, helped me with my first few written speeches, and by his excellent example, showed me how it was done properly! I always loved Table Topics, impromptu one- to two-minute speeches, where I could make stuff up on the fly! So much like short storytelling!

All of this was done without microphones. Then, on the urging of another mentor, Dr. Blaise Allen, I became an Intern to the Annual Palm Beach Poetry Festival. In addition to helping a particular Teaching Poet with administrative tasks, I was in charge of getting the class attendees on stage to read their new poems, and introduce them to using a microphone! As an added benefit, I was able to read one of my own poems. One year I got brave enough to do a

Performance Poem (told, not read) called *Mama Says*. The Director of the Poetry Festival and a famous performance poet was in the front row. I took a deep breath and told myself, "Now or never," and I did it!

It took me 13 years to write and rewrite this poem, till I found the perfect ending. *Mama Says* is a favorite of mine, and I perform it every year at 100,000 Poets and Musicians for Peace event. My Mom has passed away since I wrote this poem about her good advice: "If you can't say anything nice, don't say anything at all." My Mom was my first mentor and I honor her memory with this poem.

Performing that poem was a turning point for me. I started telling stories on stage with the Palm Beach Storytelling Guild at the annual Tellebration, a celebration of storytelling that occurs internationally the Saturday after Thanksgiving. A fun local venue for me is the Community Cabaret at the Willow Theater, Sugar Sand Park in Boca Raton. There, 19 local dancers, singers, comedians, and storytellers entertain a packed house of 250 guests. South Florida has talent!

Taking a course in fiction writing at Broward College turned into an unexpected opportunity. A classmate wrote a short story that he turned into screenplay. I got involved to make costumes for the movie. He looked at me and said, "I haven't cast the grandmother of the main character. With a wig and some makeup, you would fit the part!" Long story short, I walked the red carpet at Cinema Paradiso in Fort Lauderdale for the opening of *86 Fat Boy*. It sure was fun to play against type. In this movie, I was the evil grandmother. In real life, I am a sucker for a pouty-faced grandchild!

FEAR is False Energy Appearing Real! Many people are

afraid of speaking in public. One day, I saw a speaker frantically going over and over his speech in a car parked outside a venue. When his turn came to speak, he forgot his sequence, and became very frustrated. This got me to thinking how storytelling had helped me—the one with the good memory that is so short—remember my speeches.

I developed a method: The 3 R's of Speeches - How to Read, Write, and Rehearse a Speech in 45 Minutes or Less! (Though I spent 13 years finishing one poem, my tolerance for writing speeches tests my patience quotient!) I have guest lectured in several places teaching this method in workshop format. I am pleased to say that participants were able to prepare and give their speeches successfully in the workshops. Additionally, I have received emails and personal testaments from participants who say this method has allowed them to move forward in their speaking careers.

Ten years ago, I had the opportunity to attend Krackerjac Clown University in Delray Beach. I graduated first in my class, though that might have something to do with the fact that my initials are AA. I was already a Face Painter, and I studied Balloon Twisting, Magic (I suck at this), costuming, types of clown makeup and physical comedy. Being a Professional Clown simply added to my being a Teaching and Performing Artist. I worked with hundreds of underprivileged children in Title I after-school programs teaching Literacy through the Art of Clowning. Three years ago, I added Bilingual (Spanish or French) Puppetry to the mix. Puppets are multilingual and help shy children learn English!

I was teaching the children to make and color hand puppets. I opened my puppet's mouth and showed the kids how to make the lips, teeth and uvula. I had them look in each other's mouths to see the small dangling uvula that vibrates when you say "ah". A child raised his hand and said, "Ms. Alexandre, my puppet doesn't have a uvula cause he's a boy!" Yes, as Art Linkletter said, "Children say the darndest things!"

After losing a humor contest, I found out I wasn't as funny as I thought I was. Again, opportunity presented itself. A Meetup group, The Comedy Shack, offers classes in Plantation, FL, in a friendly, supportive venue for helping standup comedians. There I learned how to hone my comedy and went on to write and perform several winning contest entries.

Of all my speeches, stories, and clown performances, my favorite is a PowerPoint presentation, full of authentic memorabilia, about my beloved parents. My parents were Holocaust survivors. Sam and Sonia Jamnik had incredible senses of humor. They taught me that it is not enough to survive, that we must thrive. From them, I got the adage: Tragedy plus time equals humor.

Sam Jamnik and Sonia Goldman were high school sweethearts in Poland separated by World War II. After the war (1945), Dad started a soccer team for the residents of the European Refugee Relocation Camp in Berlin. One of the soccer players told Sam that he had seen Sonia. Sam went looking for her and found her! A love of soccer and a love story! I was born in that Relocation Camp a few years later. Yes, this is my favorite story!

I hope that you, the reader, will take some time to mine your own experiences for stories that will make good speeches. I highly recommend this book to help you on the path: *The Artist's Way* by Julia Cameron. I live my life in gratitude to the teachers and mentors who have helped me become a Teaching and Performing Artist. I wish for you to recognize the many opportunities that come your way.

"Not feeling motivated? Feelings follow action. Just pretend. Take action. Act as if. Surprise. NOW you're feeling it!"
~ Trish Carr

Ken Course helps thousands worldwide achieve their personal and professional goals. He is a renowned speaker and consultant, focused on helping you create results in all areas of your life.

He is the host of "Find Your Momentum," on Money 105.5 and findyourmomentumradio.com. Ken is best known for his work with bestselling author, Loral Langemeier and her company, Live Out Loud.

As the founder of Explore Momentum, Ken dedicates himself to transforming communities with a focused mix of passion and strategy. Through his innovative Momentum Model, you will explore your relationships, passions, career/businesses, creativity, health, families, and spirituality.

You can contact Ken at exploremomentum.com, kencourse.com, or (775) 434-8010.

Accidental Momentum

Ken Course

I'm actually an accidental speaker.

I often imagine having a conversation with myself twenty years ago and seeing the look of disbelief. I would never have imagined I'd be speaking three weeks out of every month. I wouldn't have believed I would work on three New York Times Bestselling books, travel around the world, or become a leader for one of the biggest financial trainers in the world. I definitely would have laughed at the idea of hosting a radio show, developing hundreds of programs and products, or working with tens of thousands of entrepreneurs on their businesses.

I have always seen myself as an artist (and still do). My highest values are creativity, integrity, and passion.

Although this is my story, I want to share what will be most valuable to you. In reading this, you're looking for hints, tips, tricks, and reinforcement that you're on the right journey.

The good news is that by reading this you *are* on the right journey. The bad news is there's no such thing as a "perfect journey."

Through my story, I want you to remember that I couldn't have told you what was happening as it happened. Fifteen years ago, I would have laughed!

Through my story, I ask you to remember the following:

- Being in service and relationship will create all your opportunities.

- Your task is to become an expert in relationship itself, not a particular subject matter or expertise.

- Relationship trumps content every time. Rapport is far more important than teaching.

- Your vision, actions, and relationships are what will keep you going when you feel like giving up.

Growing up in the Detroit area, I dreamed of creating happiness through performance. My personality and ambition didn't make much sense based on my environment, where I was surrounded by addiction, misery, and fear. My parents were too young, underequipped, and unprepared to have such a curious and energetic child. Most of my time was spent recording performances alone on a tape recorder in my bedroom and generally avoiding what was happening in my home. As with most young and difficult families, we moved often. I struggled to socialize, and simply focused on building upon my intellectual gifts.

I didn't start building relationships until high school, where I experimented with just about every form of performance. I've been a musician and songwriter since early in my life, which was only matched in intensity by my first drama performances in high school. Through the close friendships I built in theater, which were truly my first real relationships, I began to transform my life.

The most notable risk was that my friends and I formed an improvisational theater group in high school that performed around the Detroit area for two years. Night after night, we'd either be completely great or terrible, but simply enjoyed each other. Years later, my improvisational theater experience is what I draw on more than anything in my speaking. Anyone that is speaking should study and practice improvisation as it will vastly improve your speaking ability.

My tumultuous home and family life finally led me to a break from the Detroit area, opening up a number of frightening and new opportunities. At 19, I boarded a Greyhound and found myself in South Lake Tahoe, CA. My goal wasn't to build a speaking platform or even a career, but to get as far away as possible from years of pain and trauma. I worked my way through a number of odd jobs, before finding myself at a local non-profit in South Lake Tahoe.

I began my career as an administrative assistant, but due to great coaching and mentoring from the executive director of the center, I quickly grew into a program developer and manager. Most of all, my mentor valued my boisterous nature and creativity, which she allowed me to explore fully. Each day I was working with families that were similar to mine, which gave me a great deal of perspective on my own struggles in life.

The most important teaching over those years was that in solving the problems of others, I was also solving my own. Their healing was my healing. Their learning was mine as well. I also was able to lean heavily on a mentor and team when my own strength would fail. This led me into further opportunities with a local college, as well as various consulting gigs in the community service arena. When I was in service to the community, I gained more than I would have ever imagined.

In my newfound strength and accomplishment, I made one of my biggest "wrong turns." I returned to Detroit, believing I would be able to bring the "magic" home. Although I value the learning, I ended up back in Tahoe after two years feeling completely defeated. I had no idea what was next, only that I had my gifts, talents, and passion.

Again, I had made the right move without knowing.

I spent a few months back in non-profit, but a connection from years earlier sprung up that brought me into a completely new life. This connection also came from solving problems and a chance phone call. In helping a long time friend solve a technical problem, I found myself in a completely different environment.

I had never heard of the speaker I was working with, Loral Langemeier, or her company, Live Out Loud. In fact, I was pretty sure I'd found my way into some sort of strange money cult.

The "entrepreneur language" was completely new to me. I was raised to "keep my head down, work hard, and collect my paycheck," a pretty common view in Detroit. I had been behaving this way all my life – building relationships, leading teams, and developing programs – but I had never thought about these things as "marketing and sales." I also didn't see it as being particularly valuable.

I've seen this in most entrepreneurs I coach or train.

Whether you know it or not, you're impacting the world around you.

Much like the non-profit, I started behind the scenes. I was working on technical tasks, running events, developing content, and trying to learn as much as I could about this new world of entrepreneurship. However, over the years of performing in a larger role at the non-profit, I had a yearning to come out from "behind the scenes." That need was so intense that I was regularly willing to leave my position to find a place where I'd have that opportunity.

In the midst of my great frustration, I delivered my first presentations. I remember very little about them outside of the frustration, as I thought about them as dry, technical demonstrations of a software tool. The truth is, the transformation was occurring while I wasn't paying attention. I was convinced that it was the WRONG thing when it was exactly what I needed.

The "dry, boring, technical" presentations I was giving about a software tool were getting a lot of attention. This attention led to further opportunity about my marketing knowledge, the new language I had put around what I had already been doing for years.

In my mind, my first presentations were awful, but I was driven ahead by compliments, competitiveness, and new ideas. My creativity outweighed my perfectionism, and I matched Loral Langemeier's relentless drive to serve more people around the world.

Once again, in service of something else, the noise in my head felt small. On stage after stage, which seemed to get larger and larger, I transformed without really knowing. I still felt the same doubt, anxiety, and worry. I simply had to trust that I was giving everything I had and remember that I was there for the people in front of me, not myself.

In many books, the "magical transformation" seems to get jumped. It goes from "1 to 100" with a phrase or two. In my story, it's 10 years that all boils down to a few simple statements:

- Persistence is everything. I took every speaking opportunity, large or small, on any topic – even ones I didn't love!

- I always show up in service to others, which in turn serves me.

- The "magical transformation" has taken 15 years of learning, practicing, and refining my message.

Despite all my accomplishments, I still feel like a beginner in my craft. Every day is a new mystery and I show up with the most openness I possibly can. I'm willing to fail and fail often.

In the beginning, I imagined that most of these sayings were used-up clichés. It's easy to dismiss motivation and inspiration as a fad. It's easy to dismiss the thousands of people that'll tell you the same things about positivity, persistence, and passion. You might read this book passively and think, "Not me."

I was definitely the "not me." I could just be a troubled kid from Detroit, which I actually am.

Ten years and thousands of engagements later – maybe those clichés are on to something after all.

Velma Alford is a wife, mother and grandmother. She is a speaker, author and founder of Lighten Up All Over, LLC. Velma received her Bachelor of Arts degree in Transpersonal Education. She is a Light Language teacher, a T.A.T.® Certified Professional and Trainer, and an Accelerated Change Template (ACT) ™ facilitator. Velma's most sacred passion and mission is assisting others in getting to the core of what needs healing then creating ripple effects of generational healing, health, and joy.

You can contact Velma at (225) 715-9268, velma@lightenupwithvelma.com, www.lightenupvelma.com, and Facebook at Lighten Up.

A New Pair of Glasses

Velma Alford

The first time I was called upon to speak was in second grade. I can see myself on that dreadful day. I had recently needed to wear glasses and had chosen a pair of pink "butterfly" glasses with the swooped up sides. I was so proud of them and I loved how I looked in them. The day my teacher Mrs. Becnel called on me to come to the front of the class and read, I pranced, feeling confident and pretty. As I began to read, some of the students laughed at me, making fun of my glasses. I crumbled. I don't remember the teacher taking up for me or shh-ing the students. My confidence deflated, my shoulders drooped, and I swear I could feel my throat tighten up. I felt embarrassed, hurt and alone. With my head down, I finished reading and then walked to my desk. As a child growing up in an abusive home where freedom of speech barely existed, I soon learned I was not safe to be seen and heard.

From that day forward, standing and speaking in front of a group made my knees weak, my heart race, my voice crack...if anything came out at all.

Even during a small acting part in a junior high school play, I totally forgot my lines and no one stepped up to prompt me. In college, I was required to take Speech. I dreaded every assignment that required a speech or having to get up in front of the class -- prepared in advance or impromptu. I'd feel weak and lightheaded. The speeches I enjoyed the most were when I could demonstrate something -- a how-to of some kind. When my hands were busy and people had something to focus on other than me, I felt safer, more relaxed and not alone. Those visual aids were powerful allies.

Over the course of my older adult life as a speaker, I continued to measure my worthiness and success by the reaction, real or imagined, of the audience. Anytime that I had to "perform" in front of others, my gut and throat would tighten up and my mind would go blank. Yet, all this time, there was a deeper strength and desire brewing inside me. My soul had a vision; it had a voice and it had a lot to say with great courage, confidence, enthusiasm, and inspiration. I had messages within me that needed to be shared through speaking and writing.

In 2009 I enrolled in online teleclasses to become an ordained licensed interfaith angel minister. Over and over people would comment about my voice and how soothing it was. I was called the velvet voice of God. Over and over people would give me compliments about how their lives were changed and how they felt so safe listening to my messages. They told me about their new found courage to vulnerably express their long-unexpressed experiences, thoughts, and feelings.

Slowly I stopped obeying the critical voice within and began believing what the people I cared about helping were telling me. One by one, I stretched and took small risks speaking in front of others. As my confidence grew, I gave myself encouragement and permission to speak up more.

I became a CASA (Court Appointed Special Advocate) volunteer for children who have been removed from their homes due to neglect and abuse. As I gave hope to the desires and needs of these children, my own inner voice and desires gained clarity and strength.

I am still a very young speaker, learning to trust myself and let my guard down when speaking to others in groups. What I have now that I didn't have then is the gentle, encouraging, loving, and professional support and guidance of Coaches in Women's Prosperity Network -- Nancy Matthews, Trish Carr, Susan Weiner and Sandra Hanesworth. The more time I spend with them, and with the Women's Prosperity Network community, the more I learn, the more my confidence builds, and the more I feel safe to allow my soul's messages to bubble up and be voiced.

I am no longer that 6-year-old little girl standing alone in front of the group expecting to be sneered at, with no one to encourage and believe in me. I am a powerful, beautiful, passionate woman who has the support in place to go as far and as high as I could ever imagine.

When people say nice things about me, I begin to let that in as fuel to keep my desires pumped and alive. The Women's Prosperity Network founders, mentors, and community are amazing. The forums inspire me, and everyone, to call our highest and best selves forward. I am eternally grateful for these opportunities to grow beyond my wildest imagination!

With my mentors' higher vision in this new territory for me, I am overcoming my fear of public speaking, and I am learning how to share my message and my services. I now know that I have so many people whose expertise in public speaking can take me into my next best experience as a budding speaker and author.

Participating in the Business of Speaking Intensive Training, sponsored by Women's Prosperity Network, was a quantum leap for me. Prior to coming to the training, my left shoulder had been hurting and the pain progressively got more excruciating while I was in the training. I had to be taken to the emergency room by my kind and loving roommate, Ellen McDowell. As I was getting help, I came to understand that, metaphysically speaking, my speaking fears from the past had been stored in my left shoulder. I am left handed and this pain represented my stuckness and inability to experience life with joy. My deep-seated sadness and heaviness from that day in second grade were rising to the surface to be healed, acknowledged, and released. I am now choosing to allow my experiences as a public speaker to be loving, kind, joyful, and inspirational.

More and more I am willing to change and open my heart and my voice to express my messages and purpose. I am here to share. I am now able to speak up and express myself with ease.

I am now inspired to take the stage and speak because I know that, as I break through my fears and limiting beliefs, I gain courage and confidence, which gives others like me who have a burning desire to help, permission to step up and step out. I know what it's like to be afraid to speak for fear of being laughed at, or because my message differs from someone else's. I am committed to making changes within myself and helping others do the same so their messages can be heard and their dreams, desires, and goals can be realized.

In order for my business to grow and for me to reach others with my messages, I need to keep my sights on the highest good and keep myself in the company of leadership that has mastered the art of building and maintaining structures for success.

As I am now beginning to step onto the stage, I sometimes return to the scared little girl who wants to run away and hide. But with the ongoing encouragement and confident guidance I am receiving, I am choosing to stay on this path and take the stage one step at a time.

Each time I speak in front of groups, I feel my confidence getting stronger and my messages becoming clearer. I feel more comfortable and relaxed. The people who attend my presentations, and teleclasses, are inspired to trust themselves and the process too in taking their own personal next right and best step. I am learning that the speaker in me is unique and is emerging. My fears of not being as good as someone else are diminishing each time I speak.

My first client from a speaking engagement has become a lifelong friend that I care deeply about and am so proud of -- myself. For the past 50 years, we have worked together healing, learning, practicing, and growing into the person I am becoming, discovering and fine-tuning the messages that long to be shared. This is a lifelong experience of epic proportions.

For now, speaking in front of groups is still new and somewhat uncomfortable, yet even with the butterflies, nervousness, and excitement, I can see and feel progress being made in so many areas -- trust, confidence, clarity, and safety.

As you consider your own journey to the stage, I

recommend that you join and surround yourself with people who are already master speakers, who encourage you to take one more step forward, and who honor the length of every step. That way you can grow in safety and trust as you embark on this journey. Trust the wisdom of those who have successfully gone before you. I encourage you to acknowledge every success you make, big or small, because they are all big.

My mission continues to be finding my voice, speaking my truth, and helping others to Lighten Up All Over. I am wearing a new pair of glasses!

"It's really all about perspective and choices. They determine the quality of your life and the level of success you have." ~ Susan Wiener

Lauri Hunter, a native "Yankee" from Connecticut, has always been a *Do It Scared – Walk by Faith and Not by Sight* kind of person. With a background in Court Reporting, Insurance, Phlebotomy and Training, Lauri is always full of big ideas to match her big smile and intends to serve the world with the same big, bright intensity. This speaker, author, singer, songwriter, and coach is a single parent of two amazing young adult children, who are just as enthusiastic about life. She also is a caregiver for her mother, who has been an incredible influence in her life. They are her "why" that fuels her ODOO© (Opening Doors Of Opportunity) attitude. She is the Chief Executive Inspirational Officer of The Motivating Factor, LLC, Heartfelt Hands Family Services, and Air of Inspiration.

Lauri can be reached at:
www.themotivatingfactor.com;
lauri@themotivatingfactor.com.

Knock, Knock . . . Who's there? . . . Opportunity!

Lauri Hunter

"You came out of the womb talking!" says my Mom, lovingly. What a way to start my journey...right?! I've always loved people, loved to serve and loved to communicate; however, my public "speaking" debut came differently...I sang my story from a very early age. I started singing from around age three years old. My first encounter in front of an audience was great because I was in control and every eye and ear was focused on me. My audience consisted of every Barbie Doll and stuffed animal I owned, and I was the teacher in the front of the room! I'm sure my first "real" audience was my church as I did the traditional Easter speech. It is amazing how uninhibited we can be as children, and how vigorously we embrace new endeavors and challenges.

As I grew and found myself serving in various capacities, I would find myself in the position to be in front, or speaking up in front of a group, and being the one to ask the question that everyone had in class, but no one would ask. Yet I still didn't pick up on the fact that maybe I should speak publicly for a living. I believe the closest my thoughts would go towards that end was to be a teacher and stand in front of a classroom. Surely, that would be an acceptable way to manage my strong voice and talkativeness. I was so very different from my two older siblings. They were both studious and quiet. I was compared to them often by adults. I looked a lot different, and my personality was enormously different. Thank God for a Mother full of wisdom, understanding, affection and vision. Her assurance that it was okay to be different, and cultivating the gifts that were in me, carried me a long way through many of those doubtful times.

My "Ah-Ha moment" was a series of things intertwined together. I had gotten very involved in this one particular church, and one day a visiting preacher came to church and asked me to come up front. He told me that I would be speaking before thousands of people and their lives would be changed. Well, at the time, I was in my mid-twenties, and that was way beyond my scope of imagination, and I respectfully told him he was mistaken. Imagine the gasp that echoed throughout the congregation. Plus, women having that much authority was frowned upon in that setting. I was the singer, choir director, wife, pianist, NOT the speaker. I did not realize then that I was being groomed by a source much bigger than I.

This grooming became more and more apparent as I would share my story and my journey with my congregation during a time of service called "testimony service". That was a time to share an experience or victory you had that day, week, or month. I was faithful to this process because I found it strengthening and cathartic for me. It gave me an opportunity to be publicly grateful, no matter what things looked like. As I shared, others made it clear that I was continually inspiring them and my words were giving them encouragement and hope! That was good enough for me for a long time. Though deep down I knew there was something greater for me, I was being diminished in my psyche by being around louder voices that didn't value women, getting divorced after I found myself in a verbally abusive marriage, and ultimately, a "One Time ONLY" physical encounter. I promised myself that I would never find myself in that position again! This experience birthed the title of my series: "Once Is Enough." I had this huge personality, huge heart, huge purpose all squashed up, because I allowed others to put me in the size box they felt comfortable having me in. Words have power, and keeping my singing roots close, I learned a song that quoted the Prayer of Jabez. One part said "enlarge my territory", and that's indeed what began to happen in my life.

All of us have factors in our lives that move, shape and shake us into action. My motivating factor was the love of my faith and my family and my heart to serve; hence, I named my business The Motivating Factor, LLC. My territory started being enlarged as I found my long lost friend...my voice, strong and vibrant. I found myself in front of small groups, and counseling people in my home and on the phone. It was enlarged as I left my job and a week later (two months before I was going to move my mom from Connecticut to Florida to be closer to me as she was getting older) when my mom suffered two strokes, which left her a full-care patient. I brought her and my brother into my home to care for full-time, while continuing to raise my two children as single parent. Through these very circumstances, exceptional, loving, giving, intelligent people, friends and situations entered my life to bring me to this very moment!

My route has been full of curves, yet I've found that common thread that has shown up all along…my purpose and my power…my Motivating Factor, to love, to serve, and to communicate, whether through song, through writing, or through speaking publicly to groups or one on one.

I often think of that preacher that came through town. One day I hope I can find him and tell him he was right, and thank him for being bold enough in that environment to tell me what he saw in me even though it went against the grain.

Will every speech be perfect? No, and, hey, if doctors can continue to "practice" medicine, I figure I can continue to "practice" speaking! Each of our stories are so important. I am reminded of a Bible passage that says, "They overcame by the word of their testimony…" Every time I can share my story, I believe it makes me an overcomer time after time after time. There are doors waiting to be opened, filled with opportunities every day. I look forward to fulfilling my journey and ODOOing it (Opening Doors Of Opportunity) together with all those I serve, as a Maven of Motivation and your ODOO© Expert! Those of you journeying to the stage, "Welcome! And see you at the mic!

"Among the things you can give and still keep are your word, a smile and a grateful heart." ~ Zig Ziglar

Marie Cantone is a multifaceted, results-oriented doer who brings her passion for helping people to the different facets of her life. Her diverse background and experience in the disparate worlds of insurance and marketing provides her with a unique perspective and excellent "listening and reasoning" skills, all of which set her apart in the fields that she occupies today. Marie is a licensed insurance professional who helps families achieve peace of mind by educating them on how to protect themselves and their families. She is a sought-after speaker and has been published in New York Parent Magazine. Marie is a dedicated volunteer holding positions on nonprofit boards. She was the recipient of the "2010 Outstanding Volunteer of the Year." Marie's love of volunteering and passion for helping people with special needs were the catalyst for founding the nonprofit organization, Changing Hands.

You can contact Marie at info@MarieCantone.com, 631-433-0656, or www.OurChangingHands.org.

Now is YOUR TIME to Awaken Your Dreams!

Marie Cantone

When we're young, we all have hopes and dreams. I know I did. We talk about what we want to do when we grow up. Like many little girls who are considered to be part of the era of the "baby boomers," I wanted to be a teacher or a nun. During my childhood, women weren't encouraged to have a career. Many of us were "groomed" to get married and have babies. Basically, the mindset of most young girls and women during that time was "go with the flow and make it work out."

Somewhere along the line, I lost sight of my dreams. Thinking back, I often wonder what dreams I really had or when I stopped dreaming. Did I ever really dream? When did I decide that "going with the flow" was the right thing for me? Having made the conscious or unconscious decision to ride life's waves and to land on whatever shore that wave dropped me on, I would do the best I could. Where did those messages come from? And, why did I believe them? Whose idea was this "stay home and make babies" thing anyway?

So, not knowing the answers to any of those questions and not having any real idea on how to do it differently at that time in my life, I did the traditional things. I got married, I had a baby, I got divorced, I went back to school and then I built my own life and career. I remember going to my job in marketing every day and seeing a building being built with someone's name on it. I also remember thinking, "I want my name on a building" so somewhere in the back of my mind, there was a dream that I didn't quite understand.

Like most people, I had my fair share of successes and some failures along the way. I was content or at least I "sold" myself on the idea of being content, yet I didn't really feel it. One day something happened that rattled my world. A relationship I was in at the time ended. I quit my job at the same time to start my own business and, without realizing it, I was thrown into a tailspin. I remember feeling like my feet could not hit the ground; it was like being on a trampoline. I was almost 50! This was the age when everyone was settled and knew where they were going. And here I was, once again at a place of starting over. I needed to re-engineer my life and didn't know how. In all honesty, that was the BEST thing that ever happened to me. I often reflect back and say, "THANK YOU" for that experience. I WOKE UP! I now realize that *every* experience I have had has been for a reason and brings me to a place of gratitude every time!

My journey of self-discovery had begun. Of course, therapy was the FIRST thing I turned to in my quest to understand what happened and to learn more about myself and who I really was. In the process, I started to step into my power and began doing things that I *wanted* to do. Previously, I had often been doing what I thought I *should*. Of course, as I was taking this journey of self-discovery, I was mindful of how my choices would affect the people I loved, yet the choices I made were those that were also best for me. I NOW understood I have a choice. At times, it was a difficult and painful process yet, at the same time, most rewarding.

I started searching for the meaning of life and how the world around me was part of me. With expanding mindfulness, I started a meditation practice. Then a friend of mine told me about *Momentum Education,* a company that offers transformational workshops, and through a series of what I would now call "divine interventions" I took the class.

That's where my life changed! One of the exercises was to answer the question, "WHAT DO YOU WANT?" In response, I said the typical things that most people would say: "I want to be happy." "I want to be healthy." "I want to have money." "I want a loving relationship." "I want my family to be happy." Then, out of my mouth came these words: "I want to talk in front of the United Nations" and "I want to write a book." Where that came from was beyond me. I actually looked around and wondered who said that. I was *shocked!*

Sometimes our dreams are buried so deep inside us, we don't even know they are there or what they are until something happens to wake them up!

That experience was a pivotal point in my life. Finally, my dreams were coming to life. I started to really get in touch with the KNOWING that I was born to do something special. More importantly I had a responsibility to the world to share that "something special" and to step into my power. I realized that I matter! With that realization comes great responsibility. There were, and still are, people waiting for me and I had been travelling the "safe" road which no longer worked for me.

I always wanted to leave the world a better place. When I'm gone I want people to say, "Marie made a difference." All of the thoughts that somehow got lost in daily living came to life. I was ON FIRE!! I still am!! I had no idea what that something "special" was. I just continued on the journey of self-discovery and became open to what the universe was telling me.

As part of these transformational workshops, students are encouraged (well, more than encouraged) to make declarations of things they are going to do that are a real stretch from where they currently are, things out of their comfort zone. Things that made them get the butterflies. There is NO more playing safe and small. I said I would hold an event for special needs children. Mind you, I said this around Christmas and had ABSOLUTELY no idea what I was going to do, how I was going to do it, where it would take place, and it was Christmas! I was in panic mode going from thought to thought. Nothing felt quite right, but I trusted it would come. Trusted? I didn't know what it meant to trust. Trust was so unfamiliar to me, yet trust has become a huge part of my life.

Like most great ideas, it came to me in the shower. I was to set up an organization for children and adults with special needs. They would volunteer in the community. OMG!!!! That was the best thing I ever heard. It combined two of the things I'm passionate about. The first is being of service to the community. The other is my love for people with special needs.

I remembered being in high school where we put together an event for young children with special needs, and I fell in love with the most adorable toddler with Downs Syndrome. She was a handful and, at the same time, she was incredibly charming and totally loveable! Decades later, I got involved with Special Olympics, which then led to my being on the board and volunteering at Camp Northstar, which is truly a magical experience. That was it! In that moment, I realized that this was the "something special" I was to bring to the world!

All the things I had been doing and saying were wrapped up in this vision. I immediately moved forward, having NO idea of exactly what I was doing. I still don't. The difference is that now I trust I will know exactly what I need to do. Interestingly, I realized that when something is "right", there is no struggle, and miracles seem to happen.

I founded a nonprofit organization called Changing Hands. The approval process was much shorter than expected and all of the pieces are coming together. People continue to appear as I am ready for them to support my vision as I move to the next level, which is to become a global organization. My intention in doing so is to demonstrate to the world how people with special needs are contributing, vital parts of society. AND...that is how I will get to the United Nations!! It all makes perfect sense now.

I have no doubt this project has been divinely inspired. I have been chosen to lead this organization. Yes, the fear of not being enough shows up occasionally. The difference is I now know in my heart and in my soul I am enough. I matter! I DO make a difference, and this organization WILL be my legacy.

The life I have now is nothing like the life I previously had. I've also stepped into my adventuring spirit... I've flown a plane, climbed a telephone pole, performed improv (comedy), danced and sang like a crazy lady on stage and have done so many other wonderful things. I'm giving life to all the things I NEVER could have imagined doing when my dreams were buried deep within my soul.

I invite you to find your passion! Find what lights you up and sets you on fire! Now is the time to awaken your dreams! Whether you are 20 or 60 or 70 or even 80! Do it for yourself... share your special gifts with the world and create your legacy! I did it in my 60's and I am totally ON FIRE!

"Not only are you responsible for your own life, but doing the best at this moment puts you in the best place for the next moment." ~ Oprah Winfrey

Sheril Jalm has a passion for working with individuals and businesses through both of her businesses. She helps clients strategize for their retirement through her affiliation with the John Hancock Financial Network. Sheril and her business partner, Rebecca Rosado, own Innovative Minds Consulting, LLC, consulting with clients to review their organizational processes and implement practical solutions to increase their profit. Sheril also speaks at seminars to educate the public on various financial and business topics.

Contact Sheril if you would like her to speak at your event or company: Sheril@imc-solutions.com, (561) 843-0726, LinkedIn: Sheril Jalm

Taking a Risk, Believe in Yourself!

Sheril Jalm

Standing in front of the classroom, I could feel my throat constricting and my mind going blank. What was I doing up here? Everyone was staring at me, and one student was yawning. Tears rolled down my cheeks as all my insecurities bubbled up. I was not popular. I was the kid that always had my nose in the books. I just knew everyone was laughing at me. I could not get a word out about my speech on Amelia Earhart. I was petrified.

I had a loving and understanding teacher who let me sit down and compose myself. She even let me give her the speech after school. I was extremely shy and didn't easily make friends when I was in elementary school. This experience laid the ground work for my self-image that I wasn't a great speaker nor a leader.

However, growing up in the U.S. Air Force and constantly moving every two to three years caused me to become more outgoing. I realized that I liked to be around people and learned to make friends quickly. This didn't mean I was ready to speak in front of people. I just developed friendships quickly.

The greatest gift my parents gave me was the lesson of self-reliance. My parents did not have the money to provide for us anything beyond the basics (love, food, clothing and a roof over our heads). I learned early to earn my own money. I sold gift wrap and magazines, started babysitting at 11 years old and worked two part-time jobs at 16 years old while finishing high school. I had to pay for my own field trips, school activities, car, gas and insurance. I knew early on that I had to meet specific goals in order to get what I wanted.

My journey to change my self-image started in high school. I had a great English teacher who helped me develop my writing skills and self-confidence. She provided guidance to me on going to college. She helped me set goals for myself to qualify for college scholarships since my parents did not have the money to send me to college. I had to find a way to achieve my goal of going to college. I grew up believing it would be my salvation from a life of poverty.

One of the goals was to be an officer for my high school class and join a club so I could join the National Honor Society. My grades were not a problem. I needed to be involved with school activities and decided that being Treasurer would be the least public role that I could run for. The problem was I had to run for office, completely throwing myself into the one situation that I avoided at all cost. I had to speak in front of my class and tell them why I would be the best Treasurer. My friends helped me put up posters and hand out flyers. I wrote my speech and practiced for days on end. I wound up reading my speech and hiding behind the podium. It was not my best performance, but delivered because I had a goal and understood it was a step I needed to take. I became class Treasurer which led to my acceptance in the National Honor Society. I developed a great high school resume and became the recipient of a full-tuition college scholarship (President's Award) through the State of Florida college system, as well as the Florida Academic Scholarship.

Flash forward and I'm lying in a ball on my couch full of self-doubt. How did I get here?

I had worked very hard to obtain what I had perceived was a dream job in senior management and was earning more money than I had ever dreamed of. I worked even harder and believed I was on my way up the ladder, but I was miserable. I found I did not love sitting in an office, spending my days attending meetings and not seeing daylight. The final kick was when one of the executives told me that he didn't see me ever making it to executive management. I was crushed and found myself believing again that I was not good enough. I always believed that things happen for a reason, and sometimes it's just the kick in your pants that you need to change. Although I didn't realize it at the time, being laid off from this job became the best thing to happen to me.

Now unemployed and lying on my couch in a ball of great self-pity, I knew this couldn't continue. I had always relied on my ambition to succeed and overcome obstacles. I realized it was time to brush myself off and get over my perceived failures. The lay-off wasn't about me. It was about the company needing to downsize and restructure the business.

I had to look introspectively and ask myself what I could learn from this situation. What did I do that led me down the wrong path instead of getting me what I wanted? What additional work had to be done so I would be good and ready for the new challenge? I realized that my fear of speaking in front of a group was limiting my career in Finance. This was going to be a real challenge for me as I had always dreamed of owning my own business and needed to take the steps to get there. However, I knew that, to run my own business, I must overcome my fear of speaking in front of a group and learn how to sell and communicate my passion and knowledge.

I started my own practice with the John Hancock Financial Network to help people financially strategize for their future and retirement. I started to attend networking events to learn from other entrepreneurs. I heard about the Women's Prosperity Network (WPN) and attended one of their mastermind workshops. Before long, I looked forward to the workshops and attended sessions in Ft. Lauderdale, Boca Raton, West Palm Beach and Stuart, all in Florida. I joined as a lifetime member. I was inspired by the three founding sisters, Nancy, Trish and Susan. I attended the 2014 Prosperity UN-Conference and joined the WPN coaching program because I realized this program was what I was searching for to help me improve my skills and become a successful entrepreneur. Included in the coaching program is The Business of Speaking training. I attended the training and not only did I learn a process for developing my speeches, I learned how to engage the attendees and get the sale. With a process, I gained confidence that I could be successful at speaking.

I recently started a new business with my long-time high school friend, Rebecca Rosado, as a result of attending "Three Days to Cash" with Loral Langemeier. Now I know that I have to overcome my fears if I am to be successful at both businesses.

Since the training, I have spoken at six events. I was told by many of the attendees that I am a very good presenter, and that they looked forward to attending other events organized by me. One person was a retired Human Resources Director who stopped me to share that I was one of the best presenters she has seen over the years. My success rate at gaining clients through my seminars has doubled. I am now focused on presenting at seminars to share my passion for educating on retirement and financial planning topics as well as business improvement strategies.

Recently, I had a client tell me that she has worked with many people over the years, but that day in my seminar she felt a connection. She was so impressed by my sincerity and knowledge that she knew she had to work with me. What a compliment that I would not have received before getting the right training and mentoring.

Mark Moyou is currently pursuing his Ph.D. in Systems Engineering at Florida Institute of Technology (FIT). He currently holds a B.S. in Chemical Engineering and an M.S. in Systems Engineering from FIT. Mark has been a certified personal trainer and has taught yoga for three years. He has a burning desire to teach people how to be fit within their busy lives. More importantly, he seeks to inspire the youth to live a wealthy but also healthy life.

You can find him at http://addicted2wisdom.com. He is doing his first 100 speeches for free, so check him out!

Midlife Crisis at 27

Mark Moyou

Experiencing a midlife crisis at 27! This was honestly how I felt as I told my story at my first networking event, which eventually led me to write this story. Unlike most of the *Journey to the Stage* stories, mine does not entail triumph over some life-altering adversity, but rather a more subtle beast—being gifted and indecisive. For those of you who are parents, I encourage you to meditate on my story as its lessons will surely help guide the raising of your children.

So here's my journey.

There I was sitting on the floor crying, having just gotten dumped over the phone by the "girl of my dreams". I was 23 years old, living in a foreign country working on my master's degree, with no family nearby. Months earlier, I had just begun recovering from a four–year-old shoulder injury. The pain I experienced brought me to tears at times, and it was through this that I learned the spirit-stifling effect of chronic pain. When you constantly live with pain, it becomes a part of you, and getting rid of it requires removing it from your identity. Crying is one of the most effective ways to release emotional and, in some cases, physical pain. Most pain is often the result of negative emotions being stored in the body.

Teach your kids to cry honestly, not to whine but to grieve;

there is no faster way for getting rid of that emotional pain.

Sitting there unable to cry anymore, I saw a book on my shelf named *The Traveler's Gift* and decided to open it. After reading the first few lines, I knew that these were the words that would help me to recover emotionally and help build an even stronger self-image. I read the entire book out loud and recorded it. Whenever I felt down I listened to it, until the words came out of my mouth before I even heard them. Audio is, in my opinion, the most effective and accessible way to alter the mind. This book became my gateway drug into the world of personal development and reading. The key to my ability to listen to the same recording dozens of times and not get frustrated was the fact that I knew my mind was improving and I truly wanted to embody the material. With this new found addiction to wisdom, I found a mentor to work with. A mentor that cares about you is one of the most powerful influences in your entire life. When the time is right, a mentor has the power to mold your outlook on life.

Find events in your children's lives that have brought them sadness and offer motivational material as the solution. It will change them for the better. Show your kids how to use other people's experiences to accelerate their progress by learning from others' mistakes—and make it exciting.

At this point in my life, one year after the break up, I had become engrossed in personal development and began thinking about speaking. Enter the first reality of my situation: I am an international student, which means that working off campus is not allowed. So how would I get paid to speak? This still holds me back at some level three years later, and may continue to do so.

On this motivational journey I keep hearing "follow your

passion". This only frustrates me as I realize that my studies are not my greatest joys but are a necessary component for me to stay in America. After graduating with my master's degree and having two successful interviews with promises of jobs, here I am with no job, no seemingly useful passion and only one option, which is to get my Ph.D.

More school. Really! I must be mad, right!? My only other alternative is to return to my home country and find employment, so I bite the bullet and enter graduate school. Being a Ph.D. student, I learned very quickly how much I didn't know and my sense of reality became blurred as I began to focus on solving a problem. I have to truly dedicate myself to the task, otherwise the process is painful as I watch other people enjoy their lives, while I sit in a lab. Note that my passion is not getting my Ph.D., so I continue to explore other avenues. This is the exact opposite of what I should be doing, which is focusing solely on my problem.

Here are some of the things I did to explore my passions: giving tours, doing personal training, being a surf guide, teaching yoga, tutoring, doing event management, doing an online cooking show, and landscaping. During this time I still maintained a rigorous interest in personal development and speaking. Being in Toastmasters gave me even more confidence to become a speaker, but who would listen to a graduate student who depended on his parents for financial support?

As a parent, be extremely careful how you support your children financially. When things come too easily, children obviously don't appreciate them; but even worse, they become weak in will power because their will power never gets exercised to attain the thing they want. When children do nothing and get what they want, any chances they have for experiencing a promising future in a tough world can be destroyed.

Fast forward four years after my breakup. I am still in my Ph.D. program and still not truly passionate about my work, which popular opinion says I should fix. In reality, our passions provide us joy, and monetizing them may not always lead to a financially booming future. The world needs passion, but that passion must solve a problem and make a profit for it to truly have a huge impact. Note that I still have not found my passion and at times it breaks my heart to watch someone loving what they do and knowing that I have no clue as to what that feels like. No matter, I continue to search for this elusive passion while building my skill—this skill ensures that I have a lucrative position in the marketplace from which I can fully utilize my passion once I discover it. Our passion is often right in our faces, and it can take some time to obtain a clear definition, so stay persistent. Through this persistence, I decided it was time that I upgraded my network of people.

Enter reality check number two: I am a student getting my Ph.D. What do high profile people want from me? Disregarding this reality check, I looked into a conference in California called Secret Knock. The speakers were incredible and I had a burning desire to attend, so I offered to volunteer even if it meant I had to clean toilets. I was given the opportunity to volunteer, which led to me going to a networking event where I met Nancy Matthews. She asked me, "How would you like to be a published author by October 2015?" My heart froze. I was leaning toward saying no, but I uttered, "Yes, I would. What do I need to do?" And here you are reading my story.

This journey to the stage has reminded me to continue pushing forward even if there is no visible progress, because ultimately I will die and so will you. So do I wait for tomorrow to do what I could do today? Our tomorrows are not guaranteed and the strength we have is usually only meant to be used in that day and not for the rest of our lives. Do I think that my story matters now? It may matter a little more, but I write anyway because if one person's life could be changed from my story then my journey to this stage would have been worth it.

Mery N. Dominguez, the *Connection Doctor,* is a Life Strategist and Confidence Expert. She educates and offers inspiration through her own life-success story. As a speaker, she delivers action-taking motivation, creative tools and practical ideas for seeking purpose and connecting with confidence. Mery brings the vibrancy and flair of her Colombian roots to all types of stages. Her passion is connecting people with themselves and others. She is committed to creating stronger bonds between busy parents and their teens and is also the founder of The Academy of CLASS, the mission of which is to provide strategies and skills to youth for success and empowerment.

You can contact Mery at (786) 708-7508
www.merydominguez.com, , and
mery@parenteenmoments.com.

Set Yourself Apart: Connect from the Heart

Mery N. Dominguez

My stomach growls,
My hands are sweaty
My breathing narrows,
I think I AM READY!

As I glance at the people standing before me
A question arises, is this where I really should be?

I know there's something I get to say
Hoping the audience won't run away;
I stand in mere faith that they can relate
To the message that day I plan to convey.

Every time I take the stage, I get the jitters,
Quickly I chant to myself, "I'm no quitter."
Yes, I have a bio, and credentials that speak
But I know that the most important thing, it's not about
me,
It's really about the ones who are in front of me.

I understand that I have a story
In fact, a few stories.
Some moments of sadness and

Others of pure glory.

I take a few seconds to admire the view,
My purpose is to connect with at least a few
This can be daunting, but I let my light shine
I dig from down deep and speak from inside.

I have learned through time that we all struggle
Speaking from the stage can feel like a juggle.
My mentors have said, "The stage is the way;
Speak to the masses, you'll be okay."

My goal is to resonate, perhaps not with everyone
But I know through my story I can touch someone
I get to inspire, to motivate and teach.
That in itself is my true goal to reach.

Magic happens when you're authentic and smart
Just look from within and speak from the heart.
It is the way to connect and set yourself apart.

Reflecting on what I have experienced while speaking, I was inspired to write that poem. My friends that speak professionally say they can relate. Sought out and renowned speakers find courage within. The right mindset makes the vulnerability exciting.

For the past two decades I have been an educator. Speaking in front of the classroom is a bit different than speaking to a crowd. Yet I think I found the secret sauce. The object is not to make an impression but rather to leave an impression. It is important to disconnect from the fear and connect from the heart.

Regardless of the topic I'm speaking on, I make it relatable to my audience. Planning is imperative. I take ample time to plan using a specific formula that makes this process simple. Yet, I've learned it's important to simply speak to the audience. Not just to stand and talk, but to create an intimate conversation. Asking questions, being relevant, getting to know the audience through their expressions and their responses is very useful and fascinating. This openness and awareness makes the experience more impactful for both the speaker and the audience.

The key is to let go and be YOU. The heart is a not just an organ; it is a gift. When we share stories from the heart it is amazing how words flow. Let's say you're teaching people about investments. You still get to share your experience through a story saying what you've learned and the results you obtained. This makes you not only an expert in your trade but a master at connecting with integrity.

It is joyful to see faces that smile, eyes that widen, people that clap. Some jot down phrases that strike them while others simply stare as if they were reading your lips. I confess that at times I catch a wandering eye. However, I know not to take that personally. It's all a matter of perception. Some may be worried, going through heartaches, stomachaches, sleepless nights, or being troubled with concerns that have nothing to do with my presentation. So, why worry? I often remind myself that not everyone will be ready for my message and that's ok. I am grateful to connect with those that God put before me that will receive the message I am delivering. Those that get that enchanting

"AHA". That is truly where the gift lies.

I encourage you to let go of fear and think of the important things you need to say because you and your message matter. Show others how much they matter, too. The power of words spoken from the heart has prevented wars and can keep a nation at peace!

I vividly recall giving my first speech on building confidence. I was set to deliver "Love the One in The Mirror" to a group of about 250 women. I wrote my speech out and revamped it a few times before deeming it acceptable. I printed my speech in a large font size so I could see it from the podium while standing tall in front of my audience. When I arrived at the venue, I walked around to connect with a few people before I presented. As I was getting some of their names, I also asked a few people why they were there. Getting to meet the audience beforehand is an excellent practice that many of my mentors, including the fabulous Trish Carr, suggest. It also allows me to calm my nerves and build rapport with the audience before I am on stage.

I picked up the program to see the list of speakers. There I was! I saw my name and picture on the beautiful color program, and I was stunned! It was very enlivening. I gathered my belongings and headed toward my seat. That is when it hit me. I didn't have my printed speech! My 22-point font notes were still on my desk at work. It was a Saturday! Still in shock, I called my husband to print my speech off my computer and bring it to me. The venue was about 30 minutes away from my home. I told him I had saved the speech on my laptop. Unfortunately, my laptop was dead. What could be worse? He told me he couldn't find my charger. Turns out it was in my car.

Talk about the importance of arriving early! But at that point it wasn't early enough. The keynote speaker was about to wrap it up. I was the next one to speak. My world was tumbling down as I stood there, feeling far outside of my comfort zone. Frantic and frustrated, I spoke to my husband and he said, "You don't need the paper; you captivate people when you speak. You were made to help people because you bring out good qualities in people all the time. Everything you need to say comes from your heart."

At that moment, I felt ignited and I knew that I had to do just that, speak from the heart.

I shared my story that morning. The story of a girl who got pregnant at a young age and disappointed her father. The one who thought her world had ended during her teen years. I shared about my divorce, my life as a single mother and later finding the love of my life. I relayed the experiences that had led me to love the one in the mirror every day. I encouraged every woman in the audience to find her passion and live in her purpose. I also shared my mission to inspire and teach girls who find themselves in the position I faced when I was a teen, through my non-profit organization, Academy of CLASS, and to stimulate closer bonds between parents and their teens through my company, Parenteen Moments. As I ended my speech, everyone clapped and cheered. Seeing watery eyes and smiling faces proved to me that my husband was right. I was meant to speak.

Today, I stand tall. I enjoy the look of pride in my father's eyes, the valuable lessons that I share with my daughters, and the satisfaction everyone gets when I reach them with my words full of love and inspiration. I tell you that if the thought has ever crossed your mind, then you too are meant to speak.

I'll leave you with these five tips to set you apart:

- Pick your story and pin-point your lesson.

- Repeat your story to yourself and anyone willing to listen.

- Speaking day: Arrive early and engage with your audience before you speak.

- Be authentic *even if it means being a little strange.*

- Connect from the heart because that's where we feel.

"It's a new day! Remember it is only in the present moment that your power can be harnessed to create your future."
~ Nancy Matthews

Nansi Coughlin, RN-C, MSN, CCM, ARNP, lives in South Florida with her husband and their 16-year-old son. Her eldest son Jesse, who served 12 years in the Navy, and wife Vicki live in South Carolina. Nansi works full time in the medical profession, and part time with her Mary Kay business as an Independent Sales Director, mentoring women to success. Nansi is active in her church, St. Maximillian Kolbe, and volunteers every Sunday at Memorial West giving Communion and prayer to the infirm. Nansi's Nest, a home for displaced girls, will be open in 2018.

You can connect with Nansi at nansicoughlin@aol.com, www.marykay.com/nansicoughlin, or (954) 243-8409.

Step Up in Faith: Your Guardian Angel Has Your Back

Nansi Coughlin

When I was about 5, I queried my mother about something over my shoulder. Something I could not see but only feel. I realized just recently it was my Guardian Angel, the one who saved me when my pant leg got caught in the train that I hopped to the movies, the one who saved me from sure death as I stared down the barrel of a hand gun, the same one who prevented me from drowning one summer in the lake, and the one who kept me buoyant when the ice on the half-frozen lake cracked and I slipped below it. Growing up in rural Connecticut, I had a picture perfect childhood and no one could tell me that life was not perfect. At the age of ten, I could not comprehend, that in just two short years, I would be left for dead on the street, after being abducted from my home in the sleepy neighborhood of Candlewood Shores one Friday, a night I was home alone.

I spent many summers in Windsor Locks with Aunt Mary who was a nurse. I am quite sure the angelic presence which was created by her crisp clean white uniform helped formulate my life plan of becoming a nurse. Aunt Mary would take me shopping, and give me the change. I had a passion for counting the coins, squirreling them away, hoping my older brother Gary and younger sister Linda would not find them. As the middle child, I could never keep anything for myself. I marked all of my prized possessions with my name in BOLD BLACK letters. There was no question who was the rightful owner! I wanted my mom to know when something belonged to me, and only me. I counted.

Graduating at 16, I knew the power of prayer, the strength of my words echoed under the bridge I called home. Both of my children have seen my *bridge home*, tucked under I-95. I had to leave home at 15; I never told them why. It was not important. I had the strength to say no. Enough was enough. I was fortunate enough to have a summer job in Hartford Connecticut, painting the house of the Registrar for Hartford College for Women. Her name was Doreen and she was determined that I get a college education. That fall, I found myself living in a dorm, and taking Oceanography and German in college! I designed an outdoor clothing line, under my label, Tamara Wilderness, and hand sewed each garment to perfection.

The following summer I first called home a sail boat, then a tug boat, and finally a double decker bus. I soon purchased my first home, a 1957 International Harvester, and outfitted her to travel the country. School would wait. The full scholarship to Yale school of Nursing would wait. Traveling around the country, and then the world, I knew I was special. Finally, I was free from abuse, heartache and loss. I had a very simple life. I traveled for nine months with my guitar, a pair of jeans, and a couple of shirts, boots, and the wrap I needed to wear in West Africa.

It is a well-known fact that victims of abuse have difficulty with boundaries. How do we let someone in, yet protect ourselves from further abuse? Having been violated in so many areas, I knew I needed to go through therapy. I had to let go of the past. After I was able to forgive the rapist, the molester, the abusers, the attackers, I was able to live! I was free! Finally!! There are plenty of reasons for me to be angry, but so many more to be happy. I have been called a Pollyanna. But I choose happiness. So what if my glasses are pink! After

all, one cannot experience light without dark, love without loss, abundance without poverty, and life without death. To everything there is a season...and for this I am thankful.

As single mom, working two jobs and crawling my way through school, I never allowed myself to look at what I had to do, only on where it was taking me. Graduating from the University of Miami with my Master's Degree as a Nurse Practitioner was a turning point in my inner strength. I knew the accomplishment created a pillar of success, which only a handful of nurses had obtained in 1996. I was so grateful to God for the strength he gave me at a time when there seemed no way possible. The odds were against me, but my God was there for me.

Sharing my story with others is still difficult. I know that God placed me in these situations so I can help others, and I do. I extend my hand to those in need because I truly understand what it is like to be beaten unconscious, raped, given up for dead, homeless, impoverished, and abandoned. The smile that comes from my heart is one of knowing. I always reach out to the street corner peddlers, for that was me, trying to eat. I volunteer at the hospital every Sunday morning giving communion to some 30 or so people, for I know what it's like to be fearful with disease, and the uncertainty of health, in need of prayer, and someone to care. I was diagnosed with malignant melanoma at age 29, and told that I would not live to see 30. This has led me to look at other people's skin, without asking, and unashamed, for it was by Grace that I lived. I always welcome the visitors into my Wednesday night Mary Kay event, for I know what it is to be full of wonder, searching for opportunities to succeed, opportunities to make a difference, or perhaps the laughter of the "Pink Bubble."

While at a Mary Kay seminar last year, I took a photo near the domestic violence display. We were given a choice of signs to hold. I finally had the courage to hold the *victim* sign, and post it to my Facebook page, a huge step for me. I was a victim of abuse and there was nothing to be ashamed of. My team was aghast as I shared my story. They could not believe where I was and how far I have come.

Life truly is what you make of it. I can choose to be faithless or faithful. For me, I would rather take the experiences I had; they are the ones I have been given. What am I going to do with them? The lessons I have learned, and the success I have been afforded, allow me to be better and not only make *my* life better, but also the lives of those touched by my presence. There is power in prayer. There is power in the Word. There is power in Love.

I still get nervous when I have to speak in front of groups of people, but I do it anyway. I know that once I start, the jitters will dissipate, and there will be excitement as I strive to make a difference. Medicine is still my passion, but I have come to love another business. Mary Kay cosmetics gave me the platform to share my story with so many women who are in need, women looking for a chance to make a difference, women looking to make extra income, women looking to improve their self-esteem, women looking to travel, and women who want to move up the ladder of success on their terms. The fact that Mary Kay has donated 50 million dollars to domestic violence and cancer proves it's a Christian company promoting God first, family second and career third. It has solidified my decision to move up from my Independent Sales Director position, and take others with me.

My lifelong dream of opening a home for displaced girls where they can seek shelter from their storm is coming to fruition. By the Grace of God, the right people have been placed in my path. Nothing is impossible. There is Power in the Spirit, so strong it has knocked me to the ground, healed my sickness and the sickness of those around me, and made reality out of childhood dreams. I have been empowered by the presence of God, and as such, I must give back. And so I do, with love and gratitude. For "to whom much is given, much is expected."

If you want more, give more. Give of your heart, your time and your talents, and you will see the power of God working miracles in your life. In faith I am stepping up to the stage because I know my Guardian Angel has my back.

Leslie Warren is a dedicated fitness professional specializing in health and wellness coaching, personal training and group fitness classes like Zumba® Fitness, R.E.D. Warrior and her own format, Crazy 80s Cardio. She is a single mother of two brilliant boys and four fur babies. She is passionate about dance and fitness and empowering women to feel healthy and strong and beautiful at any age. Her experience with depression and self-empowerment have led her to create a unique coaching program that strengthens and heals her clients from the inside out, truly revealing that beauty doesn't have a shelf life—you can be beautiful at any age.

You can contact her at (850)778-2348 or fitnesswithleslie@gmail.com.

The Future's So Bright, I Gotta Wear Shades

Leslie Warren

Public speaking is the last thing I ever thought I was going to do. After all, speaking in front of a group of people, that's what brave people do. You know, folks who are self-possessed and confident, like starship captains, or scientists, or musicians. And that *was not* me, at least not as a child. I was that geeky little girl who always had a book in her hand and was always reading. So the thought of me volunteering to get up and speak in front of a crowd was really rather odd. I didn't talk; I just listened.

But as I grew older, I realized I had a streak of free spirit in me. As a teen and young adult, I tended to think out of the box. I didn't adhere to the fashion codes and was always a step ahead of the trends. I believed that LOVE really could heal all. I was that freaky mix of geek and granola girl. I loved mud and dirt and trees and stars and science. In a way I was fearless, or maybe in hindsight, just clueless as youth tends to be. But I'd rather like to think of it as fearless. I didn't care if I was stared at for my horrendous fashion faux pas or people shook their head at my very eclectic taste in music. I was unashamedly and unapologetically and unabashedly me. But that all changed after the birth of my first child.

Two years after my first child's birth, I found myself estranged from my son's father and devastated after a custody battle over our son. You see I'd won the battle and had custody of our son. But I'd lost the war, had to move 1100 miles from home, and move back in with my parents in what I considered a backwater little town called Tallahassee, Florida. Now for a free-spirited gal raised in the big city, that was devastating enough. But things got worse, much worse. I had this beautiful baby boy, but my sadness was overwhelming. I lived in a fog of depression. Depression so deep and strong that I had to keep a mask on 24/7 just to get through the day until the mask became me. I was numb and when I looked in the mirror, I didn't know who the hell that was looking back at me. She was an utter stranger. And not only was she a stranger, I didn't like her. But somehow, someway, somewhere the old Leslie was still in there. Underneath that mask was the spunky, funky punky gal I used to be. And when I started to see that face again, magic started to happen.

At that time, was introduced to the Law of Attraction by a friend and that's when things started to change. Slowly but surely my life started to turn around. The Law of Attraction briefly states that what you think about, you bring about. Yet it's not only what you think about that you want, it's also what you think about that you DON'T WANT. Many of us go around thinking about what we don't want and wonder why it keeps showing up. What you think about, you bring about, good or bad. Yet it wasn't until I Joined Women's Prosperity Network (WPN) and met Nancy Matthews, Trish Carr and Susan Wiener—the WPN sisters—that I really understood the Law of Attraction in action. Through WPN, I tapped back into my authentic self. I remembered that I love to travel and dance. I realized that I didn't want to spend the rest of my life working at a job that I liked yet wasn't passionate about. I tapped back into the passion that was me. I realized that I was spending all my time thinking about what I didn't want instead of what I DID WANT. I started to realize something else that I'd never noticed before too. At this time, I had starting teaching a fitness format called Zumba Fitness. And that's when I noticed it. I was on a stage, literally, teaching students fitness. I also began to see myself as my students saw me. I was a spunky, funky, punky gal who was inspiring and motivating people. How did that happen??

Well, my eyes and mind had been opened to the possibility of what could be. And what could be was that which already was, I just didn't understand that. Teachers like Judee Light, Candi Parker, Burge Smith-Lyons, and of course, Women's Prosperity Network. Judee taught me how to be fearless (again), and to let go and let God. Candi taught me that bad things can happen but they don't have to control you. Burge taught me that love really is the answer and that dolphins have more fun. And WPN and the sisters taught me that when you surround yourself with likeminded awesome women, women who are dynamic and who dream, anything can, and will, happen.

The three main lessons I've learned on my journey to the stage are so simple yet remain elusive to most of us. They are: Be authentic, stand in your personal power and take responsibility.

After all those years when the depression was like a lead blanket smothering me day and night, and night and day, I have now realized that. somewhere in there, I gave up my power and my responsibility for the outcome of my life. I stopped being me and tried to blend in. But in my search to understand what I really want and remember who I am, I've discovered that I really am that amazing, confident person who turns heads, and stands out in a crowd. I am unashamedly, unapologetically and unabashedly Captain Kirk, in glasses and purple Doc Martens boots who's "got the moves like Jagger".

So in closing, I end with this quote from Marianne Williamson:

Our deepest fear is not that we are inadequate. Our deepest fear is that we are powerful beyond measure. It is our light, not our darkness, that most frightens us. We ask ourselves, "Who am I to be brilliant, gorgeous, talented, and famous?" Actually, who are you not to be? You are a child of God. Your playing small does not serve the world. There is nothing enlightened about shrinking so that other people won't feel insecure around you. We are all meant to shine, as children do. We were born to make manifest the glory of God that is within us. It's not just in some of us; it's in everyone. And as we let our own light shine, we unconsciously give other people permission to do the same. As we are liberated from our own fear, our presence automatically liberates others.

"Without clearly defined goals, we are slaves to circumstances and daily trivia." ~ Trish Carr

Regena Ozeryansky is a Transformational Coach who helps conscious women and men to get unstuck and live more passionately! Prior to establishing her coaching business, Regena was, and still is, a Real Estate Investor, Professional Realtor and dedicated Yoga Instructor. She offers a wide range of programs and services from coaching to healing as well as energy work. Regena specializes in helping her students get unstuck and move through fear to help them live more purposefully and passionately! She is a published author, public speaker, and entrepreneur. Her book, *Vibrant Women's Wisdom,* has helped hundreds of women and men to live more authentically in their own lives.

To contact Regena, email her at RealEstateReg@gmail.com or go to her website: www.SpirtualJunkie.com.

My Journey to Many Stages

Regena Ozeryansky

Funny, I remember it vividly, like a faded shadow in the background. Yet, still I see the silhouette of the first experience. The first time I was on stage! At the sweet, innocent age of 8, I remember being in my first talent show pageant. My sister was in the teenage group, I was in the pre-teen group, and I remember the dress, my hair, and the talent routine. Although some of the experience is faded, I remember the feelings, the excitement, the frustrations, and the fears. I remember the beautiful young girl who won 1st place, a regular of sorts, kind of like a pre-Rene Ramsey look alike. If I recall correctly, the beautiful young lady was on her fourth win by the time I had just started my first crack at the stage. I remember being upset that I didn't win, having been awarded only 3rd place (as though the winning place signified my worthiness at that time), I felt like #1 was the only place to be. At that time, I thought that "stage" was the only one that existed.

I now laugh, realizing that, even at the ripe vulnerable age of 8, I was haunted with this worthiness battle playing inside the walls of my head vs. the desire to be noticed deep within my fragile heart. I did not realize at the time how damaging the negative self-talk was, nor that there even was such a thing. The stage itself did not scare me at the time; my family still reminds me to this day that, even as early as the age of 4, I was not shy and, in fact, seemed to love being the center of attention.

I recall, years later, that excitement and that fearlessness faded as did the memory of the pageant show, and I slowly preferred being behind the curtain. I remember signing up for school events, and a part of me longed for center stage, such as playing the lead roles in plays, music concerts, etc. Yet another, larger part of me wanted nothing more than to hide and crawl under the covers. I realize now, it was the stage I loved, and it was everything that the stage represented that I feared. I feared the stares, the potential judgement, and the worry of "what if my message or performance isn't enough?" And now, looking back, I think of how many times I have been on "stage" since. I can close my eyes and recreate the stage. I remember my talent competition being a baton routine that I did well, I must say. Funny how we create such big stories in our heads, at least I have, many times about flaws I thought others saw in me, only to realize they saw so much more in me than I had ever imagined up to that point.

Fast forward, a year after the pageant, I'm in the 4th grade now. I begin finding my outlet of writing and often get called to the pen and paper. People ask what my favorite subject in school is, and I consistently answer, "Creative writing." Now, here I am, working on another chapter....pretty amazing! Working on my second printed book publication, and two others consecutively!

Fast forward 10+ years later, I realize my love of yoga continues. Not clear that I wanted to teach Yoga, I was called to the teachings and decided to take the certification course. I place in the back of my mind the goal of getting certified to support and strengthen my own practice.

I close my eyes and take a big, powerful, diaphragmatic, deep breath and visualize the moment when all is silent. I am standing tall with only a narrow bright light hovering above me, and I know that it means I am front and center, the focus of attention, whether I like it or not. "I asked for this," I tell myself. With perked-up ears and wide eyes, the audience listens intently to the message I deliver. It is one of hope, intention and inspiration—one that motivates others to act on their promptings, their passions and dreams. As a result of my paralysis, the block between my head and my heart, my true desires were ignored and pushed deep below the surface of my longing and wishing. The fear settles to a comfortable tone, one that drowns out the goal or dream. Until finally, after many years of ignoring the quiet voice, I realized it had become louder and louder. Eventually, I fought back. I struggled for years with being in the shadow, my own shadow. The shadow I call the gift!

I was, you see, in a nine-month depression, too scared, lonely, and afraid to share the truth of what was happening to me at the time. In fact, I didn't even know what was happening, I just knew I was petrified. I was afraid of simple things, like driving, and eating, and even talking to my friends. I feared that people would think I was crazy if I told the truth about what I was experiencing. I was exploring the possibility of becoming a chapter leader for a local amazing women's organization at the time, and quickly realized it was important, at that time, to go behind the curtain, to take care of my needs, seek support, and guidance from people I trusted, and work through this experience in quiet, a retreat of sorts. Inward and onward I now call it. And now, I proudly and humbly live to tell about it!

I was too afraid to step into my light, for fear of being seen. For fear that I'd actually be heard or, worse, that I'd be heard and judged. Feelings of unworthiness poured through years of my being, and I hid for a long time behind the curtains of doubt until finally a tsunami of depression came caving in. It wiped out my courage and strength and brought me to my knees. It was a challenging nine months, and yet one of the most special, spectacular and, now I can see, magical times of my life. The birth of a new me emerged, a better me, a more complete me! It was a true gift I feel blessed to have experienced, one that I now feel called to share with others.

So here I am sharing with you, the reader, my journey of reaching and calling in the worlds of love and light. We all have doubt, we all have fears. It is when we each find, at the core of who we are, the courage to stand tall, speak up and share our stories that we actually create space for more love in the world. By sharing our experiences with one another, we give ourselves, and each other, permission to be honest, real and authentic about who we are. I do this in my writings, and in my workshops and classes, I do this in my public speaking and even when speaking authentically with friends. I've come to learn over the last few years that I am *often* on "the stage," the stage of life I call it—the one that shows up in my inner reflection, when I am alone in my heart, and given the opportunity for mind and heart to connect. This is my journey to the stage!

"What is your stage?" I ask. Is it a book to be published?

Or a speech you desire to give? A business to birth? Or is it a way of being? Being truthful in who you are, raising to the occasion of becoming your best selves! Embracing this gift of life, I invite you to take the plunge, taking this beautiful, powerful, sometimes unpaved Journey of Life to the Next Level!

Stand up, rise up, and stand in your own light! Living *your* truth!!! That's the Journey to the Stage. "What's your stage and what's your next step," I ask?

Welcome! The stage is yours...

Sherry Kane is the Creator and Founder of the *"I Am Complete" Woman's Club* and Retreats, and is passionate about helping women live their best lives. An Inspirational Speaker, Community Leader, Author, and Healthy Lifestyle Mentor, Sherry has created a loving and nurturing community where women can come together in a sisterhood of support to experience fun, friendship, self-care and personal development. Women from all walks of life step away from their busy lives to celebrate their femininity, womanhood and embrace who they are without judgment so they can go back into the world and abundantly give to others.

For more information about Sherry:
Facebook.com/IamCompleteWoman,
IamCompleteRetreat.com. Contact her at
sherry@sherrykane.com or 954-324-3840.

My Transformation: From Caterpillar to Butterfly

Sherry Kane

If you ask me today what my thoughts are about speaking in public, I'd say, "I have a voice, and I'm not afraid to use it." But it wasn't always that way.

I was a pretty confident kid, popular and outgoing until fifth grade, when my parents moved, I started a new school and everything changed for me. Unsure of myself in my new surroundings, I withdrew and became an introvert, shy around people and afraid to be noticed.

Middle school, already a tough gig for any kid, quickly became a nightmare, and I found myself morphing into whatever kind of person I believed other people thought I should be. High school was better. I had friends and enjoyed it, but I still wasn't living authentically. Trying hard to fit in, even it if required my being someone I wasn't, became my new normal, and I kept this up into my early forties.

It was at that time, married with two boys, that I decided I wanted to grow my home-based business, which I loved and had been doing for over a decade, into something bigger. I knew that getting out and meeting new people was going to be necessary so I decided to join different networking groups. Although it was scary for me to walk into a room full of strangers and interact with them, a voice inside told me that if I wanted to have the kind of business I dreamed of, I was going to have to do this. I quickly discovered that I was out of my comfort zone, but what surprised me was this new and very intense internal spark that kept pushing me to not just keep going to networking events but to embrace an entire voyage of self-discovery.

Over the next few years, presenting my "elevator pitch" at networking events continued to stretch me in a positive way, and it was during this time that I began attending a lot of personal and business growth seminars. As my confidence grew, it enabled me to take advantage of opportunities to give on-camera testimonials about the value I received at these events. Frequently, my voice shook because I was so camera shy, but I spoke anyway. I knew I wanted to grow, have a bigger business and become a braver and better person.

As I became more relaxed and polished at networking events, I discovered I was able to keep pushing myself to be in front of the camera. People also began telling me that I was a "natural" at speaking and that my enthusiasm and passion for what I did was inspiring to them. During this time, I invested in some key mentorship programs that encouraged me to continue to challenge myself with being seen and being heard.

As I enrolled in coaching programs, one in particular for building my personal brand, helped me discover my authentic self. I was eager to take every seminar or workshop I could that would help me build a better business and especially create a speaking career. As a result, these courses finally allowed me to free the real me, the one that went into hiding in fifth grade. As more of my true self emerged, I became happier both personally and professionally because I was no longer pretending to be someone I wasn't. It was incredibly liberating!

It was also during this time that I found a "home" with Women's Prosperity Network, and I blossomed under the love and acceptance I received from this inspiring group. Trish Carr, in particular, became my personal champion, ready to help me step more into the person I was always meant to be. From business advice to emotional support, Trish believed in me when I sometimes wasn't able to believe in myself. The information and support I received from the workshops and seminars on personal growth, combined with the guidance and encouragement I received from Women's Prosperity Network, enabled me to be more at ease with speaking to strangers at networking events and being filmed for testimonials.

Finally, the ultimate opportunity in getting out of my comfort zone appeared. I was recommended to be a speaker for a big annual holiday event being hosted in the greater South Florida area. I didn't know what to expect, but when I connected with the leader of the group, she invited me to be the keynote speaker, which would require me to get on an actual stage! Scared to death but also very excited, I said, "Yes," then immediately contacted Trish and asked her to help me craft my presentation.

What happened as a result of being courageous enough to say "Yes" to that one big opportunity is still amazing to me. I did well as the keynote speaker that day and got so much positive feedback with people telling me again what a natural I was. This gave me enough confidence to keep agreeing to do more things that made me uncomfortable, but

I enjoyed pushing myself and discovering what next "crazy" thing I might do.

A couple of years later, as I became more immersed in the community and people started to know me, I was asked by Women's Prosperity Network to be a Chapter Leader, out of hundreds of other people. This position required me to lead a group that was part of a large national organization on a regular basis, something I couldn't imagine being able to do previously. From there, I accepted an invitation to belly dance on stage as part of a group at a large women's conference, which was both thrilling and terrifying. But I knew that, in order to keep being heard on a bigger platform, I would need to be seen on a bigger platform, and I couldn't resist the fun of learning how to belly dance, something I had always wanted to do.

My commitment to challenging myself as a person and a professional continued, as I kept saying "Yes" to whatever came my way that would move me forward in my business and my life. More and more of the real me kept shining through, and I realized how long I had been living in the shadows of my life.

The biggest moment of triumph finally occurred when I was able to share the speaking stage with my husband at the Women's Prosperity Network's annual conference. As I looked out at the crowd of several hundred people, I couldn't believe how far I had come, how powerful I now knew I was and how passionate I was about finally finding my voice. At that moment, I knew I had to get my message and this movement out to other women, and I made a decision that this was my calling, and I was going to embrace it with everything I had.

Today, I am the founder of the *"I Am Complete" Woman's Club*, which celebrates sisterhood and encourages women to be the best version of themselves. People all over the country are being positively impacted by this, as they nurture all the parts of themselves: body, mind and spirit. This movement empowers women and focuses on personal growth while we learn about and immerse ourselves in health and wellness, self-care, relationships, and mindset. In finding my own voice, I am helping other women find theirs, and I believe that when a woman knows and loves herself for who she truly is, she positively affects the other people around her.

On the road of personal development and while speaking, the three biggest lessons I have learned are:

First, a community that loves and supports you for who you truly are, is invaluable. They will pick you up when you are down and cheer you on when you don't want to keep going or feel like you can't.

Second, the unfulfilled dreams you had as a child can someday be realized, even if it is years later. With the *"I Am Complete" Woman's Club*, I now have a community of soul sisters, and the added bonus is that I'm creating the same for other women.

Finally, I've learned that once you find your authentic voice and you start using it, nothing can keep you from following your passion so that you become who you were always meant to be. I know now that I am brave and strong and loving and giving, and I believe that all of those qualities are within every woman. There is a COMPLETE woman in each of us.

Knowing that people are being inspired and empowered by my speaking brings me immense joy, and it is a blessing to be able to make a difference. It is an honor and privilege to use my personal journey to help others get on their own path of being amazingly authentic, so they are free to be who they are meant to be. If each woman does that, I know the world will become a better place.

"All speakers follow and formula for their presentations ... because it works!" ~ Nancy Matthews

Michele Vismaya Rubin is on a mission to help people celebrate the deliciousness in life. Through a gratitude practice, she teaches people to savor their experiences while connecting to the lessons they are supposed to learn. She is an entrepreneur, educator, Licensed Massage Therapist and world traveler. Her friends call her Vismaya, a name she was given in India which means surprise or wonder. For her, life is full of surprises. She believes that if we don't accept the gifts life offers, they stop coming.

You can contact Vismaya at
vismaya@livingingratitudetoday.com and
www.livingingratitudetoday.com.

Changing Stages

Vismaya Rubin

At seven-fifteen each morning, a warning bell sounds, reminding me that in five minutes I will be on stage, a platform that can build or destroy, nourish or deplete with a few simple words. For the past 18 years, my stage has been a classroom, and to date, it still is. This however, was not part of the original plan. My stage was supposed to be a courtroom. I had big dreams; I was going to be the first Jewish woman President of the United States.

When I graduated from college, I went to work on a cruise ship. The plan was to save money while waiting for acceptance letters from law schools. I got letters, letters thanking me for my time and effort, but denying my admission because of low test scores. Shortly after leaving the cruise ship, I started substitute teaching at the high school one of my brothers attended. Unlike the other substitutes who were working on education degrees, I was figuring out my Plan B.

The first time I took the stage was while covering an Algebra class. After numerous explanations of the same problem to different students, I decided to teach the process to the whole class. When the next class came in, I taught the process first and then handed out the assignment. Throughout the day, many students thanked me for helping them and wished I was their permanent teacher.

At 24, I was at a crossroads in my life. My degree was basically useless, and I had not been admitted to a law school. What was I going to do? Just for fun, I sent my transcripts to the Department of Education to determine how many additional classes I needed in order to obtain a high school mathematics teaching certificate. I reluctantly went back to school and took the required courses. Then, in 1997, I began teaching at a high school where I still am today, although I no longer teach math.

Albeit, I never intended to teach, I am good at what I do. As much as I give to my students, my students give to me. Teachers do a whole lot more than pass along information on a given subject. We boost self-esteem, and sometimes we have to shatter old paradigms then create new ones for our "babies" to receive the information we were hired to deliver. Once they trust us, they are like sponges, soaking up our every word, and when we are out of integrity, they are the first to call "BS". Whatever messages I impart to them must also ring true for me.

One of my first memories that defines who I am occurred when I was seven. Wearing a black t-shirt with glittery bubble letters that read, "Never underestimate the power of a woman," I stood in the median of a busy street with my grandmother, campaigning for a presidential candidate. I did not grow up with a silver spoon in my mouth, but I always had opportunities and I have always felt lucky, or blessed (I use these words interchangeably). I never doubted that I could do whatever I set my mind to, because my personal cheering squad constantly cheered me on, telling me that I was a genius while teaching me the value of education. Even though I despised high school, skipping college was never an option; it was the next logical step in the sequence of life. What I learned early on, but never articulated until recently, is that my students say they have goals, but, in reality, their goals are more like dreams rather than something they believe is possible. I know this to be true because their actions are not leading them down the right path.

My goal has always been to get out of teaching, but I haven't found anything that affords me as much vacation time or gives me the platform to make such a difference. My goal to quit teaching turned into a dream, and I realized I was going to be a lifer. I accepted that and started looking for ways to supplement my income.

In November, 2011, the idea for GRATITUDE bags™ came to me after I attended a women's event at my friend's spa. I have had a million ideas, but this is the first one that I have stuck with. In 2012, I set up shop at local craft shows and green markets. I went anywhere that someone offered me a table. After each weekend, my students greeted me and asked me what I did over the past two days. After a while, I shared with them that I started a business. Consciously, I did it because I was excited and wanted to share my life with them and, subconsciously, because I knew they would continuously ask me about it. Without knowing it, they became my accountability partners. They knew of my travels, the birth of my nephew, and that I earned a Master's degree. They also knew when my mother had a stroke and when my grandparents died. I shared this with them because my message from the stage is that we cannot control every situation, only our responses to them. Our reactions to those events are what makes us or breaks us. I also wanted to help them cultivate the ability to see the good in all situations and appreciate the little things in life. That, by far, is more important than any subject matter. I had to show them that, in spite of what was happening around me, I was able to show up and do my job.

It is time to practice what I preach. The beginning of 2013 proved to be one giant test. Anything that could be thrown in my direction was. on Valentine's Day, my dad had part of his lung removed. Two days later, my cousin's husband was killed in a car accident. Three weeks after that, my mother had another stroke, and shortly thereafter, my aunt, who was battling cancer, went into the hospital and never left. Without a gratitude practice, I am not sure how I would have made it through the first six months of that year. My business was put on hold while I was dealing with my family matters. I was constantly releasing and letting go and looking for the good in the gravest situations. As I look back, I realize that the ability to find the light in the midst of the darkness has always been one of my gifts. Don't get me wrong; I still cry, scream and go into my cave, but I am always able to find my way out.

So what compels me to grow my business? There are a few things. For starters, I LOVE my GRATITUDE bags™ and my gratitude practice. I find the more I write, the more I have to write about. My truth is that everyone, whether they buy my bags or not, should have a gratitude practice because it keeps us out of our heads and into our hearts.

Second, I am practicing what I preach to my students: set goals and, to quote Steve Harvey: "JUMP!" By jumping, I am expanding my horizons and what is possible for my life.

These past few years, I have learned perseverance and

patience. I have taken advice from other entrepreneurs rather than trying to reinvent the wheel. So lastly, doing this gets me closer to my goal, which is to become a full-time entrepreneur.

Even though I never wanted to teach, this path has given me the ability to help teens see their greatness, set real goals, and appreciate the beauty in life. If my gratitude practice helped me through the darkest of times, it can help others as well. So now, it's time to take my teaching to a bigger stage, one where I can impact adults and teens alike. This new platform allows me to help people go through life with their eyes open, and to experience things as if for the first time. My message is still the same but with a greater emphasis on the power of gratitude.

When practicing gratitude, we can shift our mood within seconds. I say practice because life will still happen but it is our choice to look for the deliciousness in each event or the lesson we are supposed to learn, or not. By being present to what works in our lives, we open the door of opportunities and attract more of what we want. We can look at situations we are afraid of differently. For me, it's about finding the gem in the pile of rocks, and it is my intention to help others find their gems as well.

The Speaker's Profitizer

How to Deliver Presentations That Maximize Your Impact & Your Income

Discover the secret formula for delivering presentations that engage and inspire your audience to take action.

- Frustrated with presentations that don't bring the results you wanted?
- Want your audience to take action and say "Yes" to working with you?
- Learn the perfect balance of delivering quality content and having them beg for more … in a NON-SALESY way!

GET THIS FREE PROVEN PRESENTATION TEMPLATE NOW

This Presentation Template Has Been Proven to Increase Sales by 100%

With
Nancy Matthews & Trish Carr

Go to:
SpeakingforFunandProfit.com

www.ingramcontent.com/pod-product-compliance
Lightning Source LLC
Chambersburg PA
CBHW050106210326
41519CB00015BA/3845